UPGRADING TO

Microsoft® WINDOWS® 95

Step by Step

Other titles in the Step by Step series:

For Microsoft Windows 95
(available in Fall 1995)

Integrating Microsoft Office Applications Step by Step, for Windows 95

Microsoft Access for Windows 95 Step by Step

Microsoft Access/Visual Basic for Windows 95 Step by Step

Microsoft Excel for Windows 95 Step by Step

Microsoft Excel/Visual Basic for Windows 95 Step by Step

Microsoft PowerPoint for Windows 95 Step by Step

Microsoft Project for Windows 95 Step by Step

Microsoft Visual Basic 4 for Windows 95 Step by Step

Microsoft Windows 95 Step by Step

Microsoft Word for Windows 95 Step by Step

Microsoft Works for Windows 95 Step by Step

More Microsoft Windows 95 Step by Step

For Microsoft Windows 3.1
(available now)

Microsoft Access 2 for Windows Step by Step

Microsoft Excel 5 for Windows Step by Step

Microsoft Excel 5 Visual Basic for Applications Step by Step, for Windows

Microsoft Visual FoxPro 3 for Windows Step by Step

Microsoft Mail for Windows Step by Step, versions 3.0b and later

Microsoft Office for Windows Step by Step, version 4

Microsoft PowerPoint 4 for Windows Step by Step

Microsoft Project 4 for Windows Step by Step

Microsoft Word 6 for Windows Step by Step

Microsoft Works 3 for Windows Step by Step

UPGRADING TO
Microsoft®
WINDOWS® 95
Step by Step

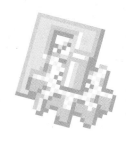

Catapult

Microsoft Press

PUBLISHED BY
Microsoft Press
A Division of Microsoft Corporation
One Microsoft Way
Redmond, Washington 98052-6399

Library of Congress Cataloging-in-Publication Data
Upgrading to Microsoft Windows 95 step by step / Catapult, Inc.
    p.   cm.
   Includes index.
   ISBN 1-55615-816-5
    1. Operating systems (Computers)   2. Microsoft Windows 95.
I. Catapult, Inc.
QA76.76.063U64 1995
005.4'469--dc20   95-10988
                                         CIP

Printed and bound in the United States of America.

1 2 3 4 5 6 7 8 9 QMQM 9 8 7 6 5

Distributed to the book trade in Canada by Macmillan of Canada, a division of Canada Publishing Corporation.

A CIP catalogue record for this book is available from the British Library.

Microsoft Press books are available through booksellers and distributors worldwide. For further information about international editions, contact your local Microsoft Corporation office. Or contact Microsoft Press International directly at fax (206) 936-7329.

Aldus and PageMaker are trademarks of Adobe Systems, Inc. America Online is a registered trademark of America Online, Inc. CompuServe is a registered trademark of CompuServe, Inc. Pentium is a trademark of Intel Corporation. FoxPro, Microsoft, Microsoft Press, MS, MS-DOS, PowerPoint, Visual Basic, and Windows are registered trademarks of Microsoft Corporation. Arial and Times New Roman are registered trademarks of The Monotype Corporation PLC. WordPerfect is a registered trademark of Novell, Inc.

Companies, names, and/or data used in screens and sample output are fictitious unless otherwise noted.

For Catapult, Inc.
Managing Editor: Donald Elman
Writer: Teresa S. Stover
Project Editor: Ann T. Rosenthal
Production/Layout Editor: Jeanne K. Hunt
Technical Editor: Brett R. Davidson

For Microsoft Press
Acquisitions Editor: Casey D. Doyle
Project Editor: Laura Sackerman

Catapult, Inc. & Microsoft Press

Upgrading to Microsoft Windows 95 Step by Step has been created by the professional trainers and writers at Catapult, Inc., to the exacting standards you've come to expect from Microsoft Press. Together, we are pleased to present this self-paced training guide, which you can use individually or as part of a class.

Catapult, Inc. is a software training company with years of experience in PC and Macintosh instruction. Catapult's exclusive Performance-Based Training system is available in Catapult training centers across North America and at customer sites. Based on the principles of adult learning, Performance-Based Training ensures that students leave the classroom with confidence and the ability to apply skills to real-world scenarios. *Upgrading to Microsoft Windows 95 Step by Step* incorporates Catapult's training expertise to ensure that you'll receive the maximum return on your training time. You'll focus on the skills that increase productivity the most while working at your own pace and convenience.

Microsoft Press is the independent—and independent-minded—book publishing division of Microsoft Corporation. The leading publisher of information on Microsoft software, Microsoft Press is dedicated to providing the highest quality end-user training, reference, and technical books that make using Microsoft software easier, more enjoyable, and more productive.

After you've used this *Step by Step* book, please fill out the feedback form in the back of the book and let us know what you think! Incorporating feedback from readers is a key component in continuously improving the books in the *Step by Step* series, and your help ensures that our materials remain as useful to you as possible.

Contents at a Glance

Table of Contents

Table of Contents

Table of Contents

*Quick*Look Guide

Customizing your display, see Lesson 2, page 38

Using shortcuts, see Lesson 2, page 31

Getting Help, see Lesson 1, page 18

Customizing your mouse, see Lesson 2, page 41

Customizing your menus, see Lesson 2, page 28

Opening recently used documents, see Lesson 1, page 12

Managing windows on the Desktop, see Lesson 1, page 13

Manipulating your windows, see Lesson 1, page 13

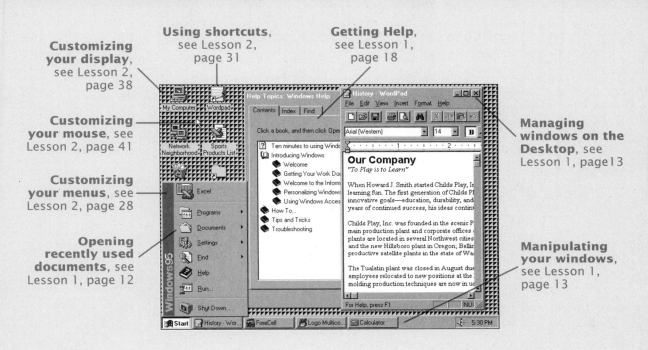

Drawing pictures, see Lesson 3, page 67

Using MS-DOS–based programs, see Lesson 4, page 87

Sharing information between programs, see Lesson 4, page 84

Writing documents, see Lesson 3, page 60

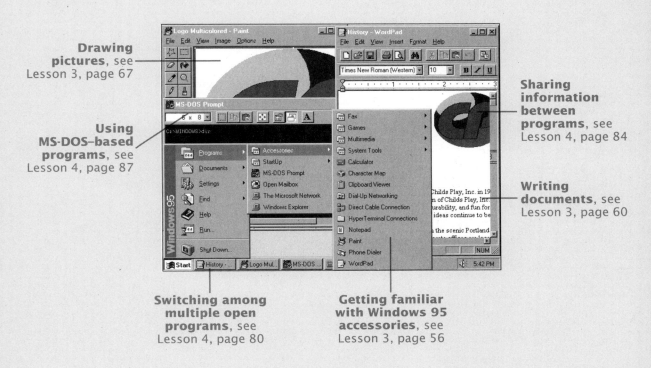

Switching among multiple open programs, see Lesson 4, page 80

Getting familiar with Windows 95 accessories, see Lesson 3, page 56

Managing disks,
see Lesson 5,
page 113

**Viewing your
filing system**,
see Lesson 5,
page 102

**Deleting
your files**,
see Lesson 5,
page 110

**Finding
your files**,
see Lesson 5,
page 116

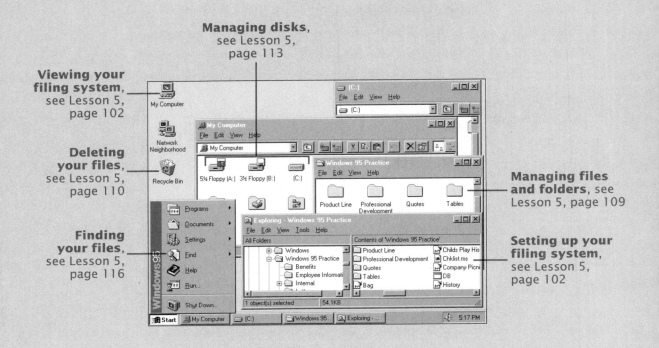

**Managing files
and folders**, see
Lesson 5, page 109

**Setting up your
filing system**,
see Lesson 5,
page 102

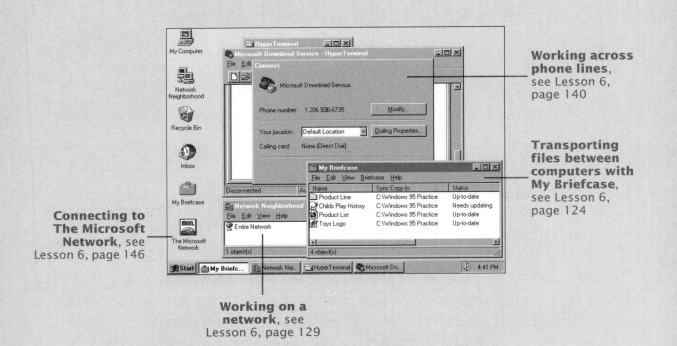

**Working across
phone lines**,
see Lesson 6,
page 140

**Transporting
files between
computers with
My Briefcase**,
see Lesson 6,
page 124

**Connecting to
The Microsoft
Network**, see
Lesson 6, page 146

**Working on a
network**, see
Lesson 6, page 129

About
This Book

In "About This Book" you will:

- Find your best starting point in this book based on your level of experience.
- Learn what the conventions used in this book mean.
- Learn where to get additional information about Windows 95.

Microsoft Windows 95 is a major revision of Microsoft Windows 3.1 and Microsoft Windows for Workgroups 3.11 that integrates the system functions of MS-DOS into a powerful, easy-to-use operating system. *Upgrading to Microsoft Windows 95 Step by Step* is designed for previous users of Microsoft Windows or Windows for Workgroups who want to quickly learn and apply the new features in Windows 95 to their work. With this book, you can learn Windows 95 at your own pace and at your own convenience, or you can use it in a classroom setting.

You get hands-on practice by using the practice files on the disk located in the back of this book. Each lesson explains when and how to use the appropriate practice files. Instructions for copying the practice files to your computer hard disk are in "Getting Ready," the next chapter in this book.

Finding the Best Starting Point for You

This book is divided into three major parts, each containing two related lessons. Each lesson takes approximately 20 to 45 minutes. At the end of each part is a Review & Practice section that gives you the opportunity to practice the skills you learned in that part. Each Review & Practice section allows you to test your knowledge and prepare for your own work.

Use the following table to determine your best path through the book.

If you	Follow these steps
Need to install Windows 95 on your computer	Follow the instructions for installing Windows 95 in the Appendix, "Installing Windows 95." Follow the instructions for installing the practice files in "Getting Ready," the next chapter in this book. For a basic introduction to Windows 95, read the section "Getting Started with Microsoft Windows 95" in "Getting Ready," and then work through Lesson 1. Work through Lessons 2 through 6 in any order.
Already installed Windows 95	Follow the instructions for installing the practice files at the beginning of "Getting Ready," the next chapter in this book. For a basic introduction to Windows 95, read the section "Getting Started with Microsoft Windows 95" in "Getting Ready," and then work through Lesson 1. Work through Lessons 2 through 6 in any order.

Using This Book As a Classroom Aid

If you're an instructor, you can use *Upgrading to Microsoft Windows 95 Step by Step* for teaching experienced Windows users about Windows 95. You might want to select certain lessons that meet your students' particular needs and incorporate your own demonstrations into the lessons.

If you plan to teach the entire contents of this book, you should set aside two days of classroom time to allow for discussion, questions, and any customized practice you might create.

Conventions Used in This Book

Before you start any of the lessons, it's important that you understand the terms and notational conventions used in this book.

Procedural Conventions

■ Hands-on exercises that you are to follow are given in numbered lists of steps (1, 2, and so on). An arrowhead bullet (➤) indicates an exercise that has only one step.

■ Characters or commands that you type appear in **bold** characters.

Print

■ You can carry out many commands by clicking the buttons at the top of a program window. If a procedure in this book instructs you to click a button, a picture of the button appears in the left margin, as the Print button does here.

Mouse Conventions

■ If you have a multiple-button mouse, it is assumed that you have configured the left mouse button as the primary mouse button. Any procedure that requires you to click the secondary button will refer to it as the right mouse button.

■ *Click* means to point to an object and then press and release the mouse button. For example, "Click the Cut button on the Standard toolbar." *Use the right mouse button to click* means to point to an object and then press and release the right mouse button.

■ *Drag* means to point to an object and then press and hold down the mouse button while you move the mouse. For example, "Drag the window edge downward to enlarge the window."

■ *Double-click* means to rapidly press and release the mouse button twice. For example, "Double-click the My Computer icon to open the My Computer window."

Keyboard Conventions

■ Names of keyboard keys that you are instructed to press are in small capital letters, for example, TAB and SHIFT.

■ A plus sign (+) between two key names means that you must press those keys at the same time. For example, "Press ALT+TAB" means that you hold down the ALT key while you press TAB.

■ Procedures generally emphasize use of the mouse, rather than the keyboard. However, you can choose menu commands with the keyboard by pressing the ALT key to activate the menu bar and then sequentially pressing the keys that correspond to the highlighted or underlined letter of the menu name and then the command name. For some commands, you can also press a key combination listed in the menu.

Notes

■ Notes or Tips that appear either in the text or the left margin provide additional information or alternative methods for a procedure.

■ Notes labeled "Important" alert you to essential information that you should check before continuing with the lesson.

■ Notes labeled "Warning" alert you to possible data loss and tell you how to proceed safely.

Other Features of This Book

- Each lesson concludes with a Lesson Summary that lists the skills you have learned in the lesson and briefly reviews how to accomplish particular tasks. You can use the summary as a quick reference guide after completing the lesson.

- The "Review & Practice" activity at the end of each part provides an opportunity to use the major skills presented in the lessons for that part. These activities present problems that reinforce what you have learned and demonstrate new ways you can use Windows 95.

- In the Appendix, "Installing Windows 95," are instructions on preparing for and installing Windows 95 on your computer.

- Also in the Appendix is the section "Matching the Exercises." In this section, you can review the options used in this book to get the results you see in the illustrations. Refer to this section of the book if your screen does not match the illustrations or if you get unexpected results as you work through the exercises.

Cross-References to Windows 95 Documentation

References to the Microsoft Windows 95 documentation and online Help at the end of each lesson direct you to specific chapters or Help topics for additional information. Use these materials to take full advantage of the features in Windows 95.

Online Help

The Help system in Windows 95 provides a complete online reference to Windows 95. You'll learn more about the Help system in Lesson 1, "Working with Windows 95."

Introducing Microsoft Windows 95

This user's guide includes information about setting up and starting Windows 95, using the Help system, and working with the operating system. It also provides explanations of the operating system's features.

Getting Ready

In "Getting Ready" you will learn:

- How to start Microsoft Windows 95 and copy the practice files to your computer hard disk.
- About the differences between Windows 3.1 and Windows 95.
- How to quit Windows 95.

This chapter of the book prepares you for your first steps into the Microsoft Windows 95 environment. You will start Windows 95 and install the practice files that come with this book. You'll get an introduction to the new Windows 95 interface as well as a review of some useful Windows techniques that might be familiar to you from using Microsoft Windows 3.1 or Microsoft Windows for Workgroups 3.11.

If you have not yet installed Windows 95, you'll need to do that before you start the lessons. For instructions on installing Windows 95, see the Appendix, "Installing Windows 95," located toward the end of this book.

 IMPORTANT   This book is designed for use with the Windows 95 operating system with a Custom setup and all components installed. If you are not sure about your setup or you need further information, refer to the Appendix, "Installing Windows 95," located toward the end of this book.

Installing the Step by Step Practice Files

The disk attached to the inside back cover of this book contains practice files that you'll use as you work through this book. You'll use the practice files in many of the lessons to perform the exercises. For example, the lesson that teaches you how to find documents stored on your computer instructs you to find and open one of the practice files. Because the practice files simulate tasks you'll encounter in a typical business setting, you can easily transfer what you learn from this book to your own work.

Copy the practice files to your hard disk

You must have Microsoft Windows 95 installed on your computer to use the practice files. Follow these steps to copy the practice files to your computer hard disk so that you can use them with the lessons.

If you do not know your user name or password, contact your system administrator for further help.

1 If your computer isn't already on, turn it on now. If you see a dialog box asking for your user name and password, type them in the appropriate boxes and then click OK. If you see the Welcome dialog box, click the Close button.

Windows 95 starts automatically when you turn on your computer.

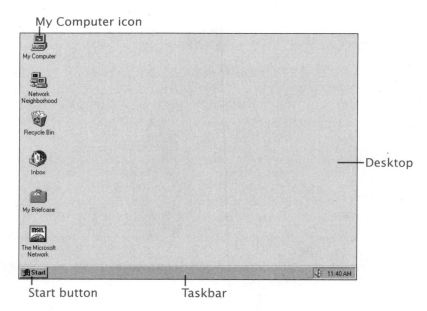

My Computer icon

Desktop

Start button

Taskbar

2 Remove the disk from the package on the inside back cover of this book.

3 Put the disk in drive A or drive B of your computer.

4 Double-click the My Computer icon to open the My Computer window.

5 In the My Computer window, double-click the icon for your 3.5-inch floppy disk drive (A or B) to open its window.

Disk drive

6 Drag the Windows 95 Practice folder to your hard disk drive icon (usually drive C) as shown in the following illustration.

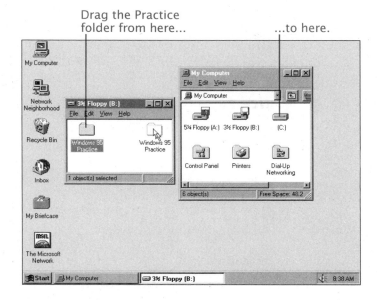

Drag the Practice folder from here...   ...to here.

While the files are being copied, you will see an animated window that illustrates the process.

7 When the files have been copied, remove the disk from your computer and replace it in the envelope on the inside back cover of the book.

You'll need to remember the name of the drive and folder where the practice files are stored so that you can open a file when you are directed in a lesson.

Each lesson in this book explains when and how to use one or more of the practice files for that lesson. When it's time to use a practice file in a lesson, the book will list instructions for how to open the file.

Lesson Background

The lessons in this book are built around a scenario that simulates a real work environment, so you can easily apply the skills you learn to your own work. For this scenario, imagine that you're a new employee at Childs Play, Inc., a toy manufacturing company, and you've previously used Windows. All the computers at Childs Play have been upgraded to Windows 95. One of your first duties as a new employee is to learn how to use the new operating system. You'll learn what's new in Windows 95 and how it compares to what you already know from using Windows previously. Then, you'll use Windows 95 in your work.

In Part 1, "Going to Work with Windows 95," you'll begin to get familiar with Windows 95. You'll start programs, locate files, and use the taskbar to manage your windows.

You'll learn how to get help when you need it. And you'll customize your Windows 95 environment, just as you might decorate and arrange items in your office to enhance your efficiency and comfort.

After you're oriented and comfortable with Windows 95, you'll be ready to get to work. In Part 2, "Doing Your Work with Windows 95," you will start working with some Windows 95 programs. You will create documents with the built-in accessories called WordPad and Paint, and you'll see how you can work with multiple Windows-based programs.

Since you are upgrading from Windows 3.1 or Windows for Workgroups 3.11, you probably already have a number of files on your computer. You also will create files by going through the lessons in this book. Though you probably have an organizing scheme for your files, Windows 95 makes it even easier to organize your files for quick access. You might also need to exchange information with others in your workgroup, or with others outside your company. You will learn how to store and share your files with others in Part 3, "Organizing and Communicating Your Work."

In the remainder of "Getting Ready," you'll get an introduction to Windows 95.

What Is Windows 95?

Previous versions of Windows required Windows and MS-DOS—two separate but coordinated operating systems—to be installed on your computer. With Windows 95, you have a complete operating system that combines and improves upon all of the previous versions of Windows and MS-DOS, including the following:

- Creates the link between you, the user, and the computer hardware by providing an interface through which you can communicate with the computer.

- Serves as the base software on which a wide variety of *programs* can operate. Examples of such programs include word processors, such as Microsoft Word; spreadsheets, such as Microsoft Excel; and databases, such as Microsoft Access.

- Handles internal functions, such as managing the computer memory and coordinating information going into the computer (input) and coming out of the computer (output).

- Provides a series of *utilities*—specialized programs to manage your system—and commands that you can use to manage your files, folders, and disks.

Not only does Windows 95 handle all of the basic operating system functions, it also provides improved features and tools that you used with earlier versions of Windows, such as the following:

- A *graphical user interface*, which uses pictures, symbols, windows, and words on your screen that you control with your mouse.

- Built-in programs, including a simple word processor and a paint program.

- The ability to display several documents and run a number of programs in their own windows, all at the same time.

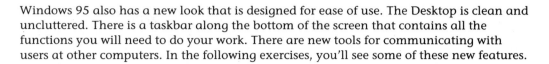

Windows 95 also has a new look that is designed for ease of use. The Desktop is clean and uncluttered. There is a taskbar along the bottom of the screen that contains all the functions you will need to do your work. There are new tools for communicating with users at other computers. In the following exercises, you'll see some of these new features.

Getting Started with Microsoft Windows 95

Microsoft Windows 95 is an easy-to-use work environment that helps you handle virtually all of the daily work that you perform with your computer. Microsoft Windows 95 also provides a common interface and common functionality among many programs—both in the way they share data and in the way you use the programs. This section will introduce you to the Windows 95 environment, and you'll learn some useful techniques for getting around Windows 95—some of which you might know from using Windows 3.1.

Start Windows 95

Starting Windows 95 is as easy as turning on your computer, and you'll be pleasantly surprised by the clean new look of the Desktop.

If you do not know your user name or password, contact your system administrator for further help.

➤ If your computer isn't already on, turn it on now. If you see a dialog box asking for your user name and password, type them in the appropriate boxes and then click OK. If you see the Welcome dialog box, click the Close button or press ENTER.

Windows 95 starts automatically when you turn on your computer.

Using Windows-Based Programs

As you probably know from working in a previous version of Windows, all Windows-based programs—the programs that are designed for use with Windows 95 or Windows 3.1—have similar characteristics in how they appear on the screen and how you use them. You'll find that many of the controls and functions in Windows-based programs are now more intuitive and easy to use. For example, the basic controls for opening and closing a window are streamlined. A major new element on the Desktop is the taskbar, which greatly enhances your ability to move between open documents and programs. In the table on the following page, you'll see procedures that you know, as well as ones that are new in Windows 95.

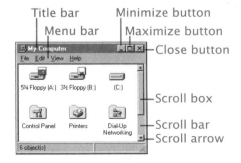

To	Do this
Scroll through a window	Click a scroll bar or scroll arrow, or drag the scroll box.
Enlarge a window to fill the screen	Double-click the title bar or click the Maximize button.
Restore a window to its previous size	Double-click the title bar, or click the Restore button. When a window is maximized, the Maximize button becomes the Restore button.
Reduce a window to a button on the taskbar.	Click the Minimize button. To display a minimized window, simply click its button on the taskbar.
Move a window	Drag the title bar.
Close a window	Click the Close button.

You'll review these Windows techniques and try out those that are new in the following sections in this chapter.

Using Menus

You'll find much that is familiar in how you use menus in Windows 95. As in Windows 3.1, when a command name appears dimmed, either it doesn't apply to your current situation or it is unavailable. For example, the Paste command on the Edit menu appears dimmed if the Copy or Cut command has not been used first. As in Windows 3.1, some commands have a shortcut key combination shown to the right of the command name. There are also many improvements in how menus appear and how commands are organized on menus.

When you installed the practice files, you probably noticed that the look of the Desktop is designed to make your work more efficient and enjoyable. In the following exercises, you'll get an introduction to Windows 95. You'll see what's new, and you'll find that what you already know about Windows will help you to get to work quickly.

Open the Edit menu

My Computer

1   Double-click the My Computer icon to open the My Computer window.

2   In the menu bar, click Edit.

The Edit menu appears. Notice which commands are dimmed and which have shortcut key combinations listed.

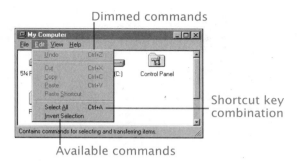

Dimmed commands

Shortcut key combination

Available commands

3 Click the Edit menu name to close the menu.

The menu closes.

Make menu selections

As in previous versions of Windows, commands on a menu are often grouped by common functions. The command currently in effect is indicated by a checkmark or a bullet mark to the left of the command name. A checkmark indicates that multiple items in this group of commands can be in effect at the same time. A bullet mark indicates that only one item in this group can be in effect at the same time. In this exercise, you'll see how the display of files and menus has been improved in Windows 95.

1 Click View in the menu bar.

The View menu looks like the following illustration.

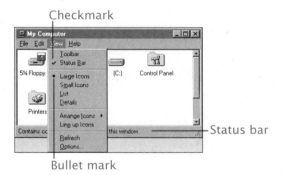

Checkmark

Status bar

Bullet mark

2 On the View menu, click Toolbar.

The View menu closes, and a toolbar appears below the menu bar.

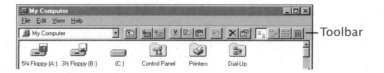

—Toolbar

3 On the View menu, click List.

The items in the My Computer window are now displayed in a list, rather than by icons.

Large Icons

4 On the toolbar, click the Large Icons button.

If you do not see the button, drag a corner of the window to enlarge it until you see the button. Clicking a button on a toolbar is a quick way to select a command.

5 On the View menu, point to Arrange Icons.

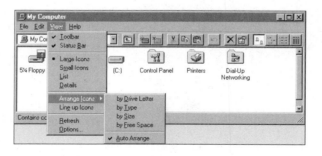

A cascading menu appears, listing additional menu choices. When a right-pointing arrow appears after a command name, it indicates that additional commands are available.

6 Click the menu name or anywhere outside the menu to close the menu.

Close

7 Click the Close button in the upper-right corner of the window to close the My Computer window.

Using Dialog Boxes

As in Windows 3.1, when you choose a command name that is followed by an ellipsis (...), Windows-based programs display a dialog box in which you can provide more information about how the command should be carried out. Dialog boxes consist of a number of standard features, with which you might be familiar, as shown in the following illustration.

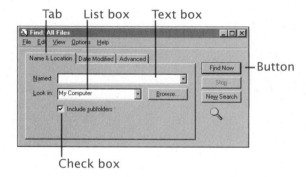

To move around in a dialog box, you click the item you want. You can also hold down ALT as you press the underlined letter. Or, you can press TAB to move between items.

Some dialog boxes provide several categories of options displayed on separate tabs. You probably used tabbed dialog boxes in Windows 3.1 or Windows for Workgroups 3.11 programs. In the next exercise, you'll see that the design of dialog boxes has been refined in Windows 95.

Display the Taskbar dialog box

1 On the taskbar, click the Start button. On the Start menu, point to Settings, and then click Taskbar.

The Taskbar Properties dialog box appears.

2 Click the Start Menu Programs tab.

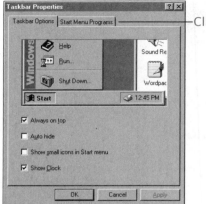
Click here.

On this tab, you can customize the list of programs that appears on your Start menu.

3 Click the Taskbar Options tab, and then click Show Small Icons In Start Menu.

Clicking a check box that is selected (that displays a checkmark) turns the option off.

4 Click the check box a couple of times, and observe how the display in the dialog box changes.

Clicking any check box or option button will turn the option off or on.

5 Click the Cancel button in the dialog box.

This closes the dialog box without changing any settings.

Quitting Windows 95

Now that you have been introduced to Windows 95, you can learn about it in more detail by proceeding with Lesson 1. To quit Windows 95 for now, you can follow these steps.

Quit Windows 95

1 Close all open windows by clicking the Close button in the upper-right corner of each window.

Close

2 Click Start, and then click Shut Down.

3 When you see the message dialog box, click the Yes button.

> **CAUTION** To avoid loss of data or damage to Windows 95, always quit Windows 95 using the Shut Down command on the Start menu before you turn your computer off.

New Features in Windows 95

Microsoft Windows 95 is significantly improved from Microsoft Windows 3.1. The changes you'll see as you work with Windows 95 are designed to make Windows easier to learn and use. The following table identifies the new features related to each lesson in this book.

To learn how to	See
Use Help.	Lesson 1
Explore the new Windows 95 Desktop.	Lesson 1
Start programs and documents with the Start button.	Lesson 1
Manage and manipulate your open windows with window controls and the taskbar.	Lesson 1
Customize your menus and Desktop.	Lesson 2
Create shortcuts to programs, folders, and documents.	Lesson 2
Give long filenames to Windows 95 files.	Lesson 3
Open and use new Windows 95 accessories, including new Desktop tools, system utilities, and games.	Lesson 3
Create and edit text documents using the new WordPad accessory.	Lesson 3
Create and edit graphics using the new Paint accessory.	Lesson 3
Find and run Windows-based programs.	Lesson 4
Start the MS-DOS Command mode and run MS-DOS–based programs.	Lesson 4

To learn how to	See
Organize your files and folders using My Computer and Windows Explorer.	Lesson 5
Move, copy, and rename files and folders using new Windows 95 techniques.	Lesson 5
Delete and recover files and folders using Recycle Bin.	Lesson 5
Synchronize files that are duplicated on different computers with My Briefcase.	Lesson 6
Share files and folders with others on your network using Network Neighborhood.	Lesson 6
Create, send, and receive mail messages with Microsoft Exchange and the Inbox.	Lesson 6
Connect to other computers through telephone lines by using Dial-Up Networking or HyperTerminal.	Lesson 6
Sign up for The Microsoft Network online service.	Lesson 6

Part 1

Going to Work with Windows 95

Working with Windows 95

In this lesson you will learn how to:

Estimated time
40 min.

- Locate and start programs using the Start button.
- Locate documents and start programs stored on your computer and on a network.
- Activate and control documents and programs using the taskbar.
- Manage and manipulate your open windows.
- Look up topics in the online Help system.

Throughout this book, references to Windows 3.1 also include Windows for Workgroups 3.11. When you start working at a new job, one of the first things you do is learn how to get around the building. You find out where the supplies are, where the coffee is, who's who, and what's the best way to get things done in your new environment. In much the same way, Microsoft Windows 95 is a new working environment for you. In this lesson, you'll learn how to get around this environment by finding programs and documents on your computer.

Because you've used Microsoft Windows 3.1 (or Microsoft Windows for Workgroups 3.11), you already have experience with a *graphical user interface*, and much of what you see in Windows 95 will be familiar. For example, you have used multiple windows on your screen, and you have used the mouse to open, close, move, and size document and program windows. Because of the many improvements in Windows 95, however, you'll be able to carry out tasks more efficiently. In this lesson, you'll explore new methods for managing your open documents and programs. You'll see what's new in Windows 95 and what's still the same.

3

Starting Programs in Windows 95

When you go to work, you use different tools and equipment to accomplish the tasks associated with your job. When you work on a computer, you use a variety of programs to create different types of documents and do different kinds of work.

In Windows 3.1, when you wanted to start a program, you had to find its group and then its icon in Program Manager. Now, in Windows 95, you can find and open programs by using the *Start button*. The Start button is located on the *taskbar* at the bottom of your Windows 95 screen, or *Desktop*.

Your screen elements might be different than the ones in this book, depending on the software and hardware you installed.

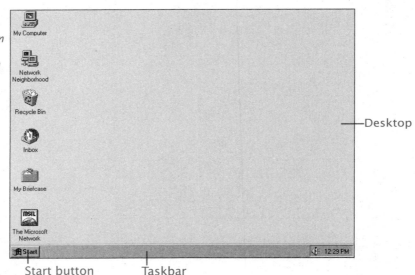

Start button   Taskbar

The Start button is your single entry point into whatever work you want to do on your computer. Whether you want to find an existing document, start a program, use an accessory, play a game, or customize your screen, the Start button can get you to the right place. It does this by presenting the *Start menu*, which gives you logical choices for your work. A nice thing about the Start button is that, unlike with Program Manager in Windows 3.1, you don't have to remember which window or program group to look in. The Start menu lays it all out for you.

Start and use a program

You'll learn more about using WordPad in Lesson 3, "Using Windows 95 Accessories."

Suppose you need to write a memo. In this exercise, you'll start WordPad, a simple word processing program that is a Windows 95 accessory, so you can see how to start a program in Windows 95.

1   Click the Start button to display the Start menu.

You can also open the Start menu by pressing CTRL+ESC.

2   On the Start menu, point to Programs.

As soon as you point to Programs, the Programs menu appears in a cascading fashion. You don't even have to click the command.

3   On the Programs menu, point to Accessories.

The Accessories menu appears to the right of the Programs menu.

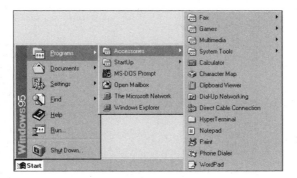

4   On the Accessories menu, click WordPad to open it.

The title of the WordPad window also appears on the taskbar as shown in the following illustration. At this point, you could write your memo.

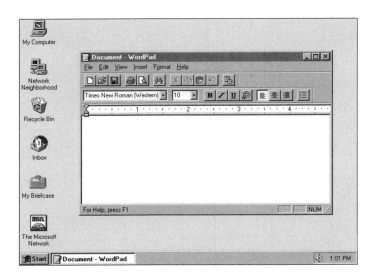

Finding Documents in Windows 95

You probably think of your work in terms of the end product, such as a letter, rather than the program that created the letter, such as Microsoft Word. In Windows 95, you can locate documents on your computer and then open them directly, without first having to find and open the program that created them. Whether your documents are stored in different folders, in different disk drives, or even in different computers on your network system, you can use one of three tools for finding them:

- Windows Explorer
- The My Computer and Network Neighborhood icons
- The Documents menu

Finding Files Using Windows Explorer

You'll learn more about Windows Explorer in Lesson 5, "Storing and Finding Files."

Windows Explorer is a refinement of the Windows 3.1 File Manager. With Windows Explorer, you can search through and open all the disk drives, folders, and files in your computer. You can also open folders and files in shared computers and other resources on your network system.

Open documents using Windows Explorer

In this exercise, you'll look for a document stored on your system that outlines the history of Childs Play, Inc. You'll use Windows Explorer to browse through your system.

1   Click Start.

The Start menu appears.

2   On the Start menu, point to Programs.

The Programs menu appears.

3   On the Programs menu, click Windows Explorer.

Windows Explorer starts. A button for this program appears on the taskbar. Windows Explorer is divided into two windows. The left window lists all the computers and disk drives that your system is actively connected to. The right window lists the contents of whatever you have selected in the left window.

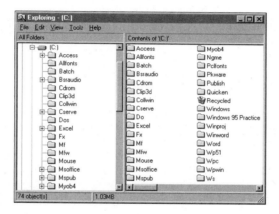

4   In the left window of Windows Explorer, titled All Folders, click the hard disk (C:).

The right window, titled Contents Of (C:), lists all folders and files stored on your hard disk.

5   In the right window, find the Windows 95 Practice folder, and double-click it. You might need to use the scroll bar to find it.

The contents of the Windows 95 Practice folder appear in the window, displaying the names of other files and folders stored there.

6   In the right window, showing the contents of the Windows 95 Practice folder, find the document called History, and double-click it.

The History document appears in WordPad. There are three buttons in the upper-right corner of every window you have opened: the Minimize button, the Maximize button, and the Close button.

You'll learn more about these three buttons in the "Managing Your Windows" section later in this lesson.

Minimize button
Maximize button
Close button

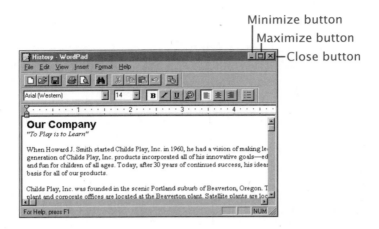

Close

Minimize

7 Click the Close button in the upper-right corner of the History document window. The History document and WordPad close.

8 Click the Minimize button on the WordPad and Windows Explorer windows.

 TIP In addition to opening documents, you can also start programs from Windows Explorer. To do this, you use Windows Explorer to find the program file and then simply double-click its name. For example, if you want to start a program such as Microsoft Excel, without opening an existing workbook, you could use Windows Explorer to find the folder in which the Microsoft Excel program file is stored. Double-click the program file name (in this case, Excel.exe), and the program opens with a blank workbook for you to start entering your data.

Getting Around in the Computer Community

In Windows 3.1, you used File Manager to browse through the files stored in your computer or network system. Windows 95 provides a new, more graphical method for displaying how the files on your computer are organized. This is done through the icons labeled My Computer, Network Neighborhood, Inbox, and Recycle Bin on your Desktop.

 NOTE If your computer system does not include an installed network, you probably will not see the Network Neighborhood icon. If your computer system does not include an installed modem with communication software, you probably will not see the Inbox icon.

My Computer

Network Neighborhood

Inbox (Microsoft Exchange)

Recycle Bin

You'll learn more about My Computer, Network Neighborhood, and Recycle Bin in Lesson 5, "Storing and Finding Files."

These icons represent your computing community. You can think of the My Computer icon as your home base, the computer on which you're actually working. When you open My Computer, you can view the folders and files that are stored on your own computer's disk drives. You can also see any other disk drives and computers on your network to which you have an active connection.

If My Computer is home base, then Network Neighborhood represents the outside community that provides different types of services to which you have access. When you open Network Neighborhood, you can view the shared folders and files that are stored on other computers in your network of computers.

You can think of Microsoft Exchange in your computing community as a combination mailbox and library. If you have telecommunication capabilities, such as electronic mail, bulletin board system access, Internet access, online services, faxing, and so forth, Microsoft Exchange keeps track of all the associated files.

Finally, Recycle Bin is your computing community's waste treatment center. When you drag a file or folder to the Recycle Bin icon, it is ready to be deleted from your disk.

View files in your computing community

In this exercise, you'll get familiar with your computing community.

1   Double-click the My Computer icon.

A new window opens, listing the icons and names of the disk drives on your computer. You'll also see folders for Control Panel, Printers, and Dial-Up Networking.

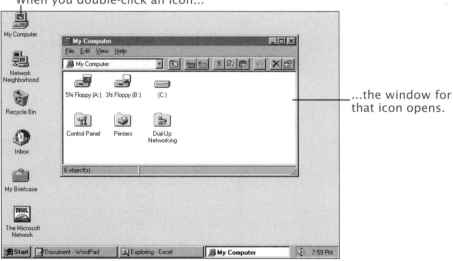

When you double-click an icon...

...the window for that icon opens.

You'll learn more about using your network later in Part 3, "Organizing and Communicating Your Work."

2 If you see the Network Neighborhood icon, double-click it. Otherwise, proceed to the next exercise.

If necessary, move the My Computer window out of the way by dragging its title bar. You'll see a list of the various computers, shared resources, disks, and public folders for your workgroup. You'll also see the Entire Network icon.

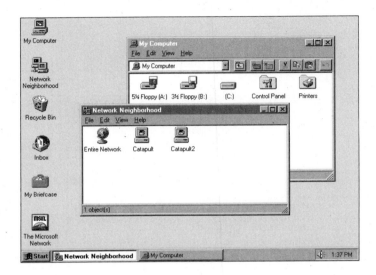

3 Click the Close button to close the Network Neighborhood window.

Change drives and folders in My Computer

Suppose you want to see the contents of a floppy disk that you have. In this exercise, you'll change disk drives to browse through the marketing files that you have on another disk.

A window is active when its title bar is highlighted.

1 Be sure that the My Computer window is active. If another window is active, on the taskbar, click My Computer.

2 Insert the Upgrading to Microsoft Windows 95 Step by Step Practice Files disk into your floppy disk drive. This is the floppy disk that came with this book.

3 Double-click the appropriate floppy disk icon (A or B) in the My Computer window to switch to it.

A new window opens displaying the contents of your floppy disk. Your screen should look similar to the following illustration.

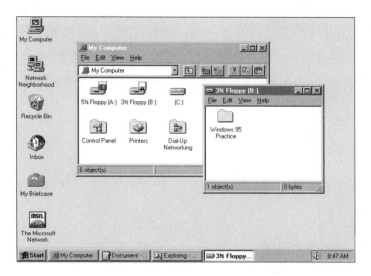

4   Double-click the Windows 95 Practice folder, and then double-click the Marketing folder icon.

A new window opens, displaying the contents of the Marketing folder. A new window opens with each new folder.

5   Close the Marketing window by clicking its Close button.

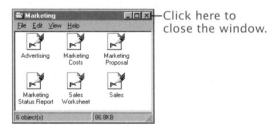

6   Close the Windows 95 Practice folder and the Floppy window by clicking the Close button in each window.

7   Remove the Practice Files disk from your floppy disk drive.

Open documents and programs in My Computer

Suppose you've been browsing through My Computer for a certain logo file. In this exercise, you'll open the logo file from a window in My Computer.

1   In the My Computer window, double-click the hard disk (C:) icon.

The hard disk (C:) window appears, displaying the names of the files and folders stored there.

11

2 Double-click the Windows 95 Practice folder.

The Windows 95 Practice folder appears, displaying the names of its files and folders.

3 Double-click the Logo Yellows file.

The Logo Yellows file opens in the Paint program, as shown in the following illustration.

You'll learn more about using Paint in Lesson 3, "Using Windows 95 Accessories."

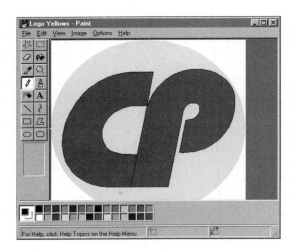

Paint is a drawing program that you can use to draw and view graphics files. Paint is provided as a Windows 95 accessory.

Opening Recently Used Documents

In the course of doing your work, you might often return to the same documents in successive work sessions. Perhaps it takes several days to complete a certain document, or maybe there are documents that you refer to while doing other work. Instead of having to search for these documents using My Computer or Windows Explorer each time you need them, you can use the Windows 95 Documents menu to open your recently used documents. The Documents menu remembers the last 15 documents you opened, regardless of where they might be stored.

Open your recent work

Maybe you want to open the History document you referred to earlier in this lesson to make a few changes and then print it. Rather than using My Computer or Windows Explorer, you'll use the Documents menu to find the document quickly.

1 Click Start. On the Start menu, point to Documents.

The Documents menu appears, listing recently opened documents in alphabetical order.

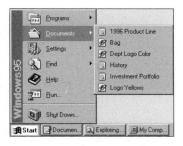

Because the Documents menu lists your own recently opened files, your menu might look different from this illustration.

2   On the Documents menu, click History.

The History document opens in WordPad. You could now make changes and print the document.

 NOTE   If you want, you can completely clear your Documents menu so that a new documents list will be created. To do this, click Start, point to Settings, and then click Taskbar. In the Taskbar Properties dialog box, click the Start Menu Programs tab; and then under Documents Menu, click the Clear button. Click OK.

Managing Your Windows

In a typical day, you might work on two or three projects at the same time. Or, you might refer to one project while working on another project. One of the most powerful features of Windows has always been its ability to have multiple programs running at the same time, each program running in its own window. In Windows 3.1, however, sometimes it was difficult to find a particular program when multiple windows were open. Other times, it was hard to find the icon of a minimized window if it was behind other windows. Windows 95 makes it easy to find all your open programs and windows, because now you have the taskbar.

The taskbar lists any open documents or programs, whether or not their windows are visible. You can use the taskbar to manipulate the various programs you are running. The taskbar is always visible on the edge of your Desktop, unless you explicitly hide it.

Manipulating Your Windows with the Taskbar

As soon as you start a program or open a window of any kind, its name is placed on the taskbar. If you open another window and then want to view the first window again, you click its name on the taskbar.

You can also manipulate your windows using the three buttons in the upper-right corner of each window: the Close, Minimize, and Maximize buttons. These buttons function in a

13

similar way to controls you used in Windows 3.1. Instead of double-clicking the Control-Menu box, you can single-click the Close button. In earlier exercises, you have already used the Close button to close windows.

In Windows 3.1, you used the Minimize box to reduce a window to an icon. In Windows 95, when you use the Minimize button, the name of the minimized window still appears on the taskbar. The window is minimized, or on "hold" as a button on the taskbar, until you need it again.

In Windows 3.1, you used the Maximize box to expand a window to fill the entire screen. The Maximize button in Windows 95 does exactly that. This is helpful when you need as much space as possible to work in a program.

Minimize, restore, and close windows

You now have several documents and programs open. In this exercise, you practice with different ways to arrange the windows on your Desktop to view what you need when you need it.

1 Be sure that the History document window is the active window on top of your Desktop. If it is not, click its button on the taskbar.

Minimize

2 Click the Minimize button near the upper-right corner of the History window.

The History window disappears, but its name remains on the taskbar at the bottom of the screen, indicating that the program is still running and the document is still open.

3 Click the Minimize button on the Logo Yellows window.

The Logo Yellows window is reduced to a button on the taskbar.

When you point to an abbreviated taskbar button, its full name appears.

4 On the taskbar, click History - WordPad.

The History window is restored as the active window on top of your Desktop. Whether a window is minimized or just behind other windows, clicking the window's button on the taskbar always brings it back to the top of your Desktop so that you can work with it again.

5 On the taskbar, click Document - WordPad.

The blank WordPad window becomes the active window.

Maximize

6 On the WordPad window, click the Maximize button.

The WordPad window expands to fill the entire screen. The Maximize button changes to a Restore button.

7 On the taskbar, click Exploring.

Windows Explorer appears on the top of the Desktop as the active window.

Restore

8 On the WordPad window, click the Restore button.

The WordPad window becomes active and returns to its previous size.

Close

9 On the WordPad window, click the Close button.

The document closes, and the WordPad program quits. The WordPad button disappears from the taskbar.

10 Quit Windows Explorer by clicking its Close button.

Windows Explorer closes. Its button is also removed from the taskbar.

TIP You can also use menu commands to manage your windows. With the right mouse button, click a button on the taskbar. A context-sensitive pop-up menu appears. The command you choose from the menu will affect the taskbar item on which you clicked.

Hiding and Showing the Taskbar

Suppose you need to see your entire page on your screen and you don't want your taskbar using up some of that screen space. If you prefer, you can hide the taskbar. This keeps your Desktop as open and available as possible. You can make your taskbar appear whenever you need it by moving your mouse pointer near the edge of the Desktop where the taskbar was "docked." The taskbar remains visible until you move the mouse pointer away from that area.

Hide the taskbar

Suppose you're working on a dense document for which you need every square inch of space on your Desktop. In this exercise, you'll hide the taskbar to give you that extra space, so you can see the entire screen.

1 On the taskbar, click History - WordPad.

2 On the History document window, click the Maximize button.

3 Click Start. On the Start menu, point to Settings.

4 On the Settings menu, click Taskbar.

The Taskbar Properties dialog box appears. This dialog box is "tabbed" at the top to let you choose between two categories of options.

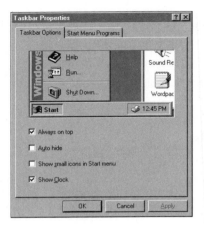

5   The Taskbar Options tab should already be active. If it is not, click the Taskbar Options tab.

6   Select Auto Hide, and then click OK.

7   Click elsewhere on your Desktop.

Your taskbar is hidden from view.

NOTE   Whenever you use the right mouse button to click an element on the Desktop, a context-sensitive pop-up menu appears, providing commands that directly affect the element you just clicked. For example, if you use the right mouse button to click an empty space on your taskbar, a pop-up menu appears that includes commands for setting taskbar properties and arranging all your windows on the Desktop.

View a hidden taskbar temporarily

When your taskbar is hidden, you still might need to use it from time to time. In this exercise, you'll bring the hidden taskbar into view temporarily.

1   Move your mouse pointer close to the bottom edge of your Desktop.

The hidden taskbar reappears.

2   Click Start. On the Start menu, point to Programs, and then click Windows Explorer.

The taskbar remains visible until Windows Explorer appears. Then the taskbar disappears again.

Show a hidden taskbar

In this exercise, you'll restore your taskbar so that it always reappears on your Desktop .

1   Move your mouse pointer close to the bottom edge of your Desktop.

The hidden taskbar reappears.

2   Click Start. On the Start menu, point to Settings.

3   On the Settings menu, click Taskbar.

The Taskbar Properties dialog box appears. Be sure that the Taskbar Options tab is active.

4   Click the Auto Hide check box to clear it, and then click OK.

Your taskbar appears again at the bottom of your Desktop.

5   On the History window, click the Restore button.

The document is restored to its original size.

Move and resize the taskbar

You can move your taskbar to any of the four sides of your Desktop. You can also make the taskbar wider if you like.

1   Move your mouse pointer to an empty space on your taskbar.

2   Drag the taskbar to the right edge of your Desktop.

The taskbar is docked along the right side of your screen. You can move the taskbar to any of the four edges of your Desktop by dragging it in this manner.

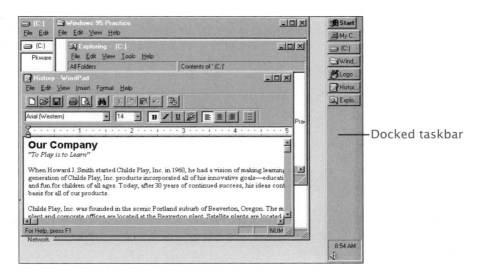

Docked taskbar

3   Drag the taskbar to the top of your Desktop.

The taskbar is docked at the top of your screen.

4   Drag the taskbar back to the bottom of your Desktop.

The taskbar is docked in its original position.

5   Move the mouse pointer to the inside edge of the taskbar so that the pointer changes to a two-headed arrow.

6   Drag the edge of the taskbar upward to widen it.

You can make the taskbar wider or narrower by dragging its inside edge.

7   Drag the edge of the taskbar downward to return it to its original size.

Getting Help with Windows 95

When you're at work and you want to find out more information about how to do a project, you might ask a co-worker or consult a reference book. When you need information about a procedure or how to use a particular feature on your computer, the online Help system is one of the most efficient ways to learn. The online Help system for Windows 95 is available from the Start menu, and you can choose the type of help you want from the Help dialog box.

For instructions on broad categories, you can look at the Help contents. Or, you can search the Help index for information on specific topics. The Help information is short and concise, so you can get the exact information you need quickly. There are also shortcut buttons in many Help topics that you can use to directly switch to the task you want to perform.

Viewing Help Contents

The Help Contents tab is organized like a book's table of contents. As you choose top-level topics, or "chapters," you see a list of more detailed topics from which to choose. Many of these chapters have special "Tips and Tricks" subsections that can help you work more efficiently.

Find Help on general categories

Suppose you want to learn more about using Calculator, a program that comes with Windows 95. In this exercise, you'll look up information in the online Help system.

1   Click Start. On the Start menu, click Help.

The Help Topics: Windows Help dialog box appears.

2   If necessary, click the Contents tab to make it active.

*Because you
have used
Windows 3.1,
you might be
interested in the
Help topics
under "Wel-
come" named "If
you've used
Windows before"
and "A List of
What's New."*

3 Double-click "Introducing Windows."

A set of subtopics appears.

4 Double-click "Using Windows Accessories."

5 Double-click "For General Use."

6 Double-click "Calculator: for making calculations."

A Help topic window appears.

7 Click the Close button to close the Help window.

Finding Help on Specific Topics

There are two methods for finding specific Help topics: the Index tab and the Find tab. The Index tab is organized like a book's index. Keywords for topics are organized alphabetically. You can either scroll through the list of keywords, or you can type the keyword you want to find. Windows 95 online Help then presents one or more topic choices.

With the Find tab, you can also enter a keyword. The main difference is that you get a list of all Help topics in which that keyword appears, not just the topics that begin with that word.

Find Help on specific topics using the Help index

In this exercise, you'll use the Help index to learn how to change the background pattern of your Desktop.

1 Click Start. On the Start menu, click Help.

The Help dialog box appears.

2 Click the Index tab to make it active.

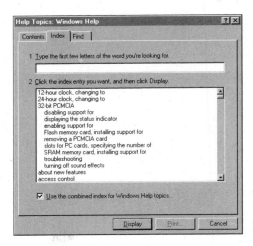

3   In the text box, type **display**

A list of display-related topics appears.

4   Double-click the topic named "background pictures or patterns, changing."

The Topics Found window appears.

5   Double-click the topic named "Changing the background of your desktop."

6   Read the Help topic.

7   Click the jump button in Step 1 of the Help topic.

Jump

The Display properties dialog box appears. If you want, you can immediately perform the task you are looking up in Help.

8   Click the Close button on the Display Properties dialog box.

9   Click the Close button on the Windows Help window.

Close

NOTE   You can print any Help topic. Click the Options button in the upper-left corner of any Help topic window, click Print Topic, and then click OK. To continue searching for additional topics, you can click the Help Topics button in any open Help topic window.

Find Help on specific topics using the Find tab

In this exercise, you'll use the Find tab to learn how to change your printer's settings.

1   Click Start. On the Start menu, click Help.

The Help dialog box appears.

2   Click the Find tab to make it active.

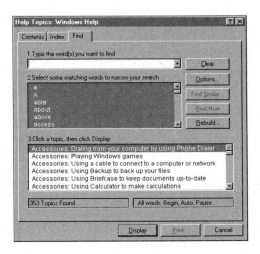

3   If you see a wizard, select the best option for your system, and then click Next. Click Finish to complete and close the wizard.

The wizard creates a search index for your Help files. This might take a few minutes. The next time you use Find, you won't have to wait for Windows 95 to create the list. The Find tab appears.

4   In the text box, type **print**

All topics that have to do with printing are displayed in the list box at the bottom of the tab.

5   In the list box under Step 3, click the "Changing printer settings" topic, and then click Display.

The Help topic appears.

6   Read the Help topic, using the scroll bar as necessary.

7   Click the Close button on the Windows Help window.

Close

21

Find Help on a dialog box

Almost every dialog box includes a question mark button in the upper-right corner of its window. When you click this button and then click any dialog box control, a Help window appears that explains what the control is and how to use it. In this exercise, you'll get help on specific elements in a dialog box by using pop-up Help.

1 Click Start. On the Start menu, click Run.

The Run dialog box appears.

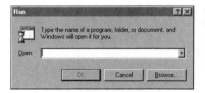

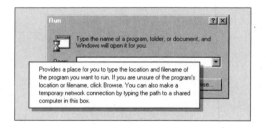

2 Click the Help button.

The mouse pointer changes to an arrow with a question mark.

3 Click the Open text box.

A Help window appears, providing information on how to use the Open text box.

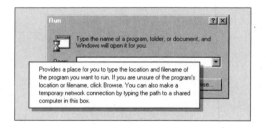

4 Click the mouse anywhere on the Desktop, or press ESC to close the Help window.

5 Click the Help button again, and then click Browse.

Help displays information about the Browse button.

6 Click Browse.

The Browse dialog box appears.

7 Click the Help button, and then click the Files Of Type list box.

The Help window appears with information about the list box.

8 Click Cancel.

9 In the Run dialog box, click Cancel.

TIP You can change the way the Help topics appear on your screen. Click the Options button in the upper-right corner of any Help topic window, and then point to Font to change the font size.

Finish the lesson

1. Close all open windows by clicking the Close button in the upper-right corner of each window.

2. If any window is minimized, use the right mouse button to click the window's taskbar button, and then click Close.

   You are now ready to start the next lesson, or you can work on your own.

3. If you are finished using Windows 95 for now, on the Start menu click Shut Down, and then click Yes.

Lesson Summary

To	Do this	Button
Start a program	Click Start, point to Programs, and then click the program name. *or* From Windows Explorer, find the program, and then double-click its name.	
Start Windows Explorer	Click Start, point to Programs, and then click Windows Explorer.	
Open a document	From Windows Explorer, find the document, and then double-click its name.	
Open a recently used document	Click Start, point to Documents, and then click the document name.	
View and open the contents of disks, folders, and files on your computer	Double-click the My Computer icon. Double-click succeeding disk, folder, or file icons.	
View and open the contents of computers, shared resources, and disks on the network	Double-click the Network Neighbor-hood icon. Double-click succeeding disk, folder, or file icons.	
Minimize a window to the taskbar	Click the Minimize button on the window.	▣
Maximize a window to fill the Desktop	Click the Maximize button on the window.	▣

23

To	Do this	Button
Restore a minimized window from the taskbar	Click the item's name on the taskbar.	
Restore a maximized window to its previous size	Click the Restore button on the window.	▣
Close a window	Click the Close button in the upper-right corner of the window.	☒
Bring an open window to the top of the Desktop	Click the item's name on the taskbar.	
Hide the taskbar	Click Start, point to Settings, and then click Taskbar. Click the Taskbar Options tab, select Auto Hide, and then click the OK button.	
Temporarily show a hidden taskbar	Move the mouse pointer close to the edge of the Desktop where the taskbar was last docked.	
Show a hidden taskbar	Click Start, point to Settings, and then click Taskbar. Click the Taskbar Options tab, clear the Auto Hide check box, and then click OK.	
Move the taskbar	Drag the taskbar to any of the four edges of the Desktop.	
Resize the taskbar	Drag an edge of the taskbar to make it wider or narrower.	
Find Help on a general topic	Click Start, click Help, click the Contents tab, and then double-click the topic you want.	
Find Help on a specific topic	Click Start, click Help, click the Index or the Find tab, type a keyword, and then double-click the topic you want.	
Find Help on a dialog box	Click the Help button on the dialog box, and then click the dialog box control for which you want help.	?

For online information about	From the Help dialog box, click Index and then type
Starting programs using the Start button	**starting, programs**
Opening documents using the Start button	**opening, files**
Using the My Computer icon	**My Computer**
Using the Network Neighborhood icon	**Network Neighborhood**
Managing documents and programs using the taskbar	**taskbar**
Manipulating windows	**window**
Referencing online Help	**Help**

For more information on	In *Introducing Microsoft Windows 95,* see
Starting programs and opening documents using the Start button	Chapter 1, "The Basics"
Using the My Computer icon	Chapter 2, "Beyond the Basics"
Using the Network Neighborhood icon	Chapter 2, "Beyond the Basics"
Managing documents and programs using the taskbar	Chapter 1, "The Basics"
Referencing online Help	Chapter 1, "The Basics"

Preview of the Next Lesson

In the next lesson, you will learn how to customize Windows 95 to make it suit the kind of working environment you prefer and to reflect the kind of equipment you use. This includes customizing your display and your mouse, and designing shortcuts to reflect your specific working habits.

Customizing Windows 95

Estimated time
35 min.

In this lesson you will learn how to:

- Access frequently used programs by adding commands to your Start menu.
- Create shortcuts to frequently used files, and display these shortcuts as Desktop icons.
- Design your Windows 95 environment to suit your preferences and the way you work.

People often tailor their work areas with an eye toward comfort and efficiency. Sometimes this involves arranging furniture, adding plants, or hanging artwork on the walls. It's also convenient to have within reach the tools, equipment, and supplies you use most often.

In Microsoft Windows 3.1 or Microsoft Windows for Workgroups 3.11, you were able to customize your Program Manager icons and groups. You could also use various tools in Control Panel to tailor how Windows looked and worked.

In Windows 95, you have similar capabilities available to change various aspects of your display, your mouse, your printer, and more. You can also create your own menus for starting programs and tailor your Desktop icons to your own preferences. In addition, you can create shortcuts to access documents and programs that you frequently use. In this lesson, you'll find out how you can create an environment in Windows 95 that is best suited to your preferred methods of working.

Customizing Your Menus

In your work area, if you use your telephone, fax machine, stapler, or tape dispenser on a regular basis, you probably have them on or near your desk for easy and convenient access. In Windows 95, you can add the command for any installed program to your Start or Programs menu. Then you always have quick access to the accessories and other programs that you use most often.

You can also remove items that you rarely use from your Start and Programs menus.

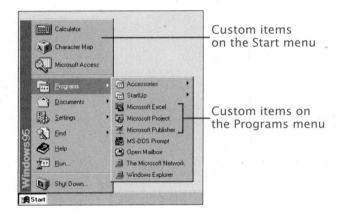

Custom items on the Start menu

Custom items on the Programs menu

Adding Commands to Your Start Menu

Adding a command to your Start menu is an efficient way to open any program you have set up on your computer system. For example, if you use the Calculator accessory often, you can add the Calculator command to your Start menu. Then, whenever you need the Calculator, you just click the Start button and then click Calculator. This is more direct than clicking the Start button, pointing to Programs, pointing to Accessories, and then clicking Calculator.

Or, suppose you have set up a new program, such as Microsoft Access, on your computer system. If you use Microsoft Access every day, it might be convenient to add Microsoft Access to your Start menu.

NOTE   Adding a command to your Start menu makes the command more readily available to you. Unlike the program icons in the Startup group in Windows 3.1, programs on the Start menu do not automatically run when you start Windows 95. See "Starting Programs Automatically" later in this lesson for more information.

Add commands to your Start menu

Character Map is a Windows 95 accessory used mainly for inserting special characters and symbols into your documents. Suppose you use Character Map almost every day. Because you're constantly referring to it, you want it to be more easily accessible. In this exercise, you'll add Character Map to your Start menu.

1 Click Start. On the Start menu, point to Settings.

Another way to open the Taskbar Properties dialog box is to use the right mouse button to click an empty area of the taskbar, and then click Properties.

2 On the Settings menu, click Taskbar to open the Taskbar Properties dialog box.

3 Click the Start Menu Programs tab to make it active.

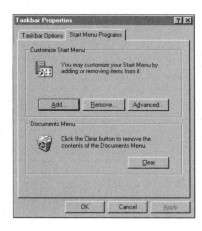

4 Under Customize Start Menu, click Add.

The Create Shortcut dialog box appears.

If you don't know the filename of a command you want to add, you can search for it by clicking Browse.

5 In the Command Line text box, type **charmap** and then click Next.

The Select Program Folder dialog box appears.

6 Click the Start Menu folder, which is the second item in the list, and then click Next.

7 When prompted for the name of the shortcut, type **Character Map** and then click Finish.

If you want to add a command to the Programs menu, you can click the Programs folder in step 6.

8 Click OK, and then click the Start button.

The Character Map command, along with its associated icon, appears at the top of the Start menu as shown in the following illustration. Items you add to the Start menu appear in alphabetical order above the default Start menu items.

You can learn
more about
Character Map
by looking it up
in the online
Help.

9 On the Start menu, click Character Map.

Character Map starts.

10 Click the Close button on the Character Map window to close it.

TIP You can also add a copy of any icon, program, folder, or file from the Desktop, Windows Explorer, or file window to the Start menu. To do this, just drag the item onto the Start button. The item's name and icon appear in the upper segment of the Start menu.

Remove commands from your Start menu

Suppose that later you decide you will not be using Character Map very often, so you don't need it taking up space on the Start menu. In this exercise, you'll remove Character Map from the Start menu.

1 Use the right mouse button to click an empty area of the taskbar.

A pop-up menu appears, listing commands for the taskbar.

2 Click Properties.

The Taskbar Properties dialog box appears.

3 Click the Start Menu Programs tab to make it active, and then click Remove.

4 In the next window, click Character Map, which is probably at the bottom of the list, and then click Remove.

You can follow
this same
procedure to
remove a
command from
your Programs
menu.

5 Click Close and then, on the Taskbar Properties dialog box, click OK.

6 Click Start.

Character Map is no longer listed as a command on the Start menu. However, you can still open it from the Accessories menu, which you open by pointing to Programs and then to Accessories.

7 Click anywhere else on the Desktop to cancel the Start menu.

NOTE You can remove only those commands that you have added to the Start menu. You cannot remove the default Start commands.

Creating Shortcuts

As part of your standard Desktop setup, you always see the My Computer and Recycle Bin icons on your Desktop. If your computer has a network system installed, you'll have the Network Neighborhood icon available to you. If you have installed modem, mail, or fax capabilities, you will probably see the Inbox icon on your Desktop.

While this setup is clean and spare, you might find it useful to add *shortcuts,* icons that graphically represent programs, folders, or documents that you use frequently. For example, you might use a spreadsheet program every day. Or, maybe you often access a certain public folder on the network. Perhaps there is a document you refer to or update every two or three days. Any of these examples is a good candidate for a shortcut that you can access directly from your Desktop.

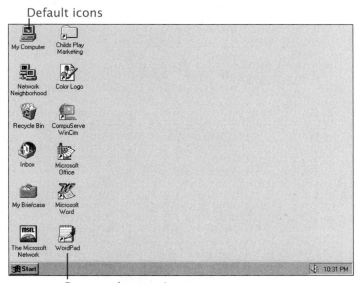

Default icons

Custom shortcut icons

A shortcut represents and functions as a pointer to the actual item, wherever it might be stored. When you double-click the icon to open the shortcut, you're opening the actual item to which the shortcut is pointing as shown in the following illustration.

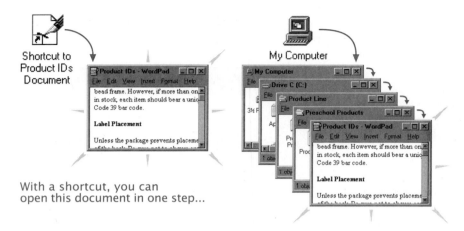

With a shortcut, you can
open this document in one step...

...instead of five steps.

Suppose you create a shortcut to a commonly used network folder. The shortcut is represented by an icon on your Desktop. A shortcut icon is identified by a little arrow in its lower-left corner as shown in the above illustration. When you double-click the shortcut icon to open it, you are actually opening the network folder, which is stored out on the network server on another computer. This is quite convenient because you save time by not browsing through drives and perhaps several folders to find the one you need.

If you decide you no longer need a shortcut, you can remove the icon from your Desktop without deleting the object to which the shortcut is pointing. You're only deleting the pointer, not the actual item.

Add shortcuts to your Desktop

In this exercise, you'll create shortcuts for three items that you use often: WordPad, the Marketing folder, and a logo graphics file.

1 Click Start. Point to Find, and then click Files Or Folders.

The Find dialog box appears.

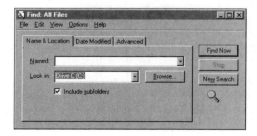

2   On the Name & Location tab, in the Named box, type **wordpad** and then click the Find Now button.

A list appears, showing all files with "wordpad" in their names.

You can quickly create a shortcut to a program file by dragging it to the Desktop with the left mouse button.

3   Use the right mouse button to drag the WordPad Application file (not the Setup, CNT, or Help file) to the Desktop.

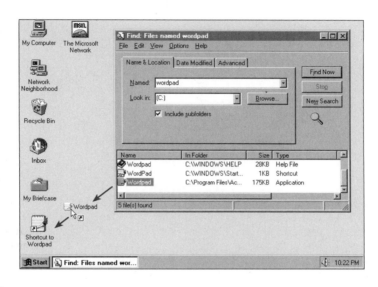

4   On the pop-up menu, click Create Shortcut(s) Here.

The Shortcut To WordPad icon appears on your Desktop.

5   Close the Find dialog box.

6   Double-click the My Computer icon, and then double-click the Drive C icon.

7   In the Drive C window, double-click the Windows 95 Practice folder.

The Windows 95 Practice folder opens.

If you drag a folder or document with the left mouse button, an independent copy of the folder or document is made on the Desktop, as represented by the icon.

8   Use the right mouse button to drag the Marketing folder onto the Desktop and then, from the pop-up menu, choose Create Shortcut(s) Here.

The Marketing folder shortcut appears on your Desktop.

9   In the Windows 95 Practice folder window, use the right mouse button to drag the Logo Multicolored file to the Desktop.

10   From the pop-up menu, click Create Shortcut(s) Here.

The Logo Multicolored shortcut appears on your Desktop.

33

Rename the shortcuts

In this exercise, you'll close the open windows, and then rename the three shortcut icons.

1   Close all open windows until your Desktop is clear of all windows.

Your screen should look similar to the following illustration.

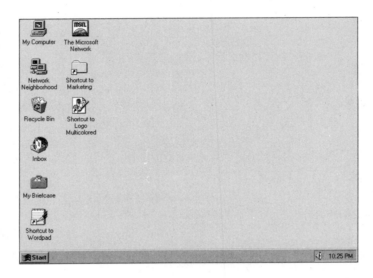

2   Use the right mouse button to click the Shortcut To WordPad icon.

A pop-up menu appears.

3   On the menu, click Rename.

The name "Shortcut To WordPad" is highlighted, and a blinking insertion point appears.

4   Type **WordPad** to replace the selection and then press ENTER.

The WordPad shortcut is renamed.

5   Use the right mouse button to click the Shortcut To Marketing folder icon, and then click Rename.

6   Type **Childs Play Marketing,** and then press ENTER.

7   Use the right mouse button to click the Shortcut To Logo Multicolored document icon, and then click Rename.

8   Type **Color Logo** and then press ENTER.

Your screen should look similar to the following illustration.

Use the shortcuts

In this exercise, you'll use the shortcuts you created to start WordPad, open the Marketing folder, and then open the Color Logo file.

1 Double-click the WordPad shortcut.

WordPad starts, as if you had started it from the Accessories menu.

2 Double-click the Childs Play Marketing folder shortcut. If necessary, drag the WordPad title bar to move its window out of the way.

The Childs Play Marketing folder opens, displaying its contents. This has the same effect as if you had opened the My Computer icon, opened the Drive C icon, opened the Windows 95 Practice folder, and then opened the Marketing folder. With the shortcut, the process of opening this folder is much quicker.

3 Double-click the Color Logo shortcut.

The Color Logo graphic opens in Paint. This is the same document that is stored in the Windows 95 Practice folder.

4 Click the Maximize button on the Paint window to see the entire logo.

5 Close all open windows, until your Desktop is clear again.

Remove shortcuts from your Desktop

Suppose that some time has passed and you're working on other projects. Because of this, you no longer need these three shortcuts on your Desktop. In this exercise, you'll delete the shortcuts using three different methods. Deleting the shortcut does not delete the item to which the shortcut was pointing.

1 Drag the WordPad shortcut to the Recycle Bin icon.

   The WordPad shortcut is removed from the Desktop and placed inside Recycle Bin.

2 Use the right mouse button to click the Childs Play Marketing folder shortcut, and then click Delete.

3 In the Confirm File Delete dialog box, click Yes.

   The Childs Play Marketing folder shortcut is removed from the Desktop.

4 Click the Color Logo shortcut, and then press DELETE.

5 In the Confirm File Delete dialog box, click Yes.

   The Color Logo shortcut is removed from the Desktop.

 TIP If you change your mind and want the deleted WordPad shortcut back, you can double-click the Recycle Bin icon to open it and then drag the shortcut onto the Desktop again. Items in Recycle Bin stay there until you explicitly empty Recycle Bin. You'll learn more about using Recycle Bin in Lesson 5, "Storing and Finding Files."

Starting Programs Automatically

In Windows 3.1, if you wanted a program to start as soon as Windows started, you added its icon to your Startup program group. In Windows 95, you can do the same thing by adding a shortcut to the program in your StartUp folder.

Find the file for a new StartUp shortcut

Suppose you like to play a game or two of FreeCell before you start working each day. In this exercise, you'll browse through your files to find the FreeCell program file. Then you can add it to your StartUp folder so that it starts automatically each time you start Windows 95.

1 Click Start. On the Start menu, point to Settings, and then click Taskbar.

   The Taskbar Properties dialog box appears.

2 Click the Start Menu Programs tab.

3 Click Add.

   The Create Shortcut dialog box appears.

4 Click Browse.

   The Browse dialog box appears. Be sure that the Look In text box indicates the hard disk (C:). If it does not, click the down arrow next to the list box, and then click the hard disk (C:).

5 Double-click Windows.

   The contents of the Windows folder appear.

6   Scroll through the list until you find the FreeCell program file.

7   Double-click the FreeCell icon.

The Create Shortcut dialog box appears again, with the FreeCell information in the command line text box.

8   Click Next.

The Select Program Folder dialog box appears.

Add a shortcut to your StartUp folder

Now that you have located the FreeCell program, you can add it to your StartUp folder. Any program in your StartUp folder starts as soon as you start Windows 95.

1   In the Select Program Folder dialog box, click the StartUp folder, which is near the bottom of the list, and then click Next.

2   In the next window, click Finish.

The Taskbar Properties dialog box appears.

3   Click OK.

4   Click Start, point to Programs, and then point to StartUp.

The StartUp menu lists any items that will start up as soon as Windows 95 starts. FreeCell is probably listed by itself.

Restart Windows 95

In this exercise, you'll restart Windows 95 and see how FreeCell starts automatically when Windows 95 starts.

1   On the Start menu, click Shut Down.

2   In the Shut Down Windows dialog box, click Restart The Computer, and then click Yes.

Windows 95 restarts with FreeCell running. If the Welcome window appears, click Close.

3   Play a game of FreeCell if you like.

Click the Help menu for details on how to play the game.

4   When you have finished, close FreeCell.

Remove a shortcut from your StartUp folder

In this exercise, you'll remove FreeCell from your StartUp folder so that it will no longer start automatically when Windows 95 starts.

1   Click Start. On the Start menu, point to Settings.

2   On the Settings menu, click Taskbar.

3 In the Taskbar Properties dialog box, click the Start Menu Programs tab.

4 Click Remove.

5 In the Remove Shortcuts/Folder dialog box, double-click the StartUp folder.

6 Under the StartUp folder, click the FreeCell shortcut, and then click Remove.

7 Click Close.

8 On the Taskbar Properties dialog box, click OK.

The FreeCell shortcut is removed from the StartUp folder.

Setting Up Your Windows 95 Environment

Although you can leave your Windows 95 environment at all the default settings, you might like to customize it to suit your own preferences. Customizing can make using your monitor, keyboard, mouse, or other hardware devices more efficient or more comfortable. Customizing can also personalize your Windows 95 world, reflecting your individual style and working patterns.

With Control Panel in Windows 95—which is similar to that in Windows 3.1—you can change the look of your display, the performance of your mouse, the date and time, and more.

Customizing Your Display

From the Windows 95 Control Panel, you can design your display like the way you decorate your office. You can choose color schemes for different window elements, such as the menu bar, the title bar, and selected text. You can choose a particular pattern for your Desktop background. To protect your monitor from possible damage caused by prolonged display of the same image, you have a wide variety of screen-saver patterns from which to choose.

Customize your display colors

Your display colors affect the background color of your display, as well as the colors of your windows, title bars, text, and other elements you see on the screen. In this exercise, you'll select a color scheme for your window elements.

1 Click Start, and then point to Settings.

The Settings menu appears.

2 On the Settings menu, click Control Panel.

The Control Panel window appears.

Another way to open Control Panel is to double-click the My Computer icon, and then double-click the Control Panel folder.

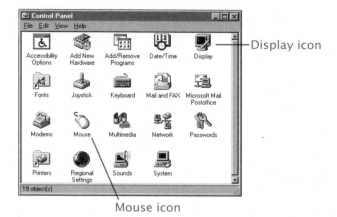

Display icon

Mouse icon

3 In Control Panel, double-click the Display icon.

The Display Properties dialog box appears.

4 Click the Appearance tab.

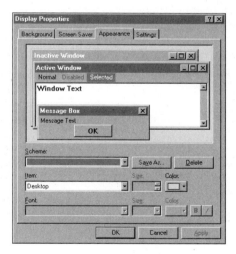

5 In the Scheme list box, click Plum (high color).

The colors in the sample display change to the Plum color scheme.

6 In the Scheme list box, click Teal (VGA).

The colors in the sample display change to the Teal color scheme.

7 Click the Apply button.

Your Desktop colors change to the Teal color scheme.

8 Sample and then select the color scheme you want, and then click OK.

 TIP If you want to change the color of an individual Desktop element, click it in the Item list box, and then select the color you want from the Color list box. You can also change Desktop element fonts, where applicable. You can create and save entirely new color schemes this way.

Choose your background

To make your Desktop background more interesting, giving yourself a more cheerful environment while you work on your computer, you can use the Display Properties dialog box to customize the background. In this exercise, you'll set the background pattern and the wallpaper, two different sets of options for the Desktop background.

Display

Another way to open the Display Properties dialog box is to use the right mouse button to click an empty area of the Desktop, and then choose Properties.

1 With the Control Panel window open, double-click the Display icon.

The Display Properties dialog box appears. Be sure that the Background tab is active.

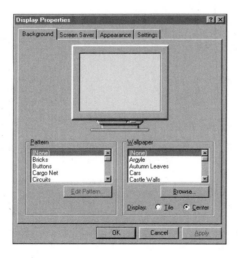

2 In the Wallpaper list box, click Argyle.

The sample shows the Argyle graphic repeated, or tiled, across the display. With Wallpaper, you usually have the choice between a repeating design tiled across the display or a single design in the center of the Desktop.

3   Click Apply.

The Argyle graphic is tiled across the sample display, and it is also on your screen display.

4   Click Center, and then click Apply to create a single design.

5   In the Pattern list box, click Bricks.

The sample display shows the Bricks pattern with the Argyle graphic still in the center.

6   Scroll downward in the Pattern list box and click Cobblestones.

7   Sample and then select the pattern or wallpaper you want, and then click OK.

NOTE   You can choose a single, centered wallpaper graphic that sits on top of your background pattern, as you've done in this exercise. However, if the wallpaper fills your screen, the pattern will be completely hidden. This is because the wallpaper always sits on top of the pattern.

Customizing Your Mouse

The way your mouse and pointer respond to your hand and finger actions helps determine the efficiency with which you can control the graphical elements in Windows 95. Perhaps you are not completely comfortable with the default settings for your mouse. With Control Panel, you can change various mouse characteristics. If you are left-handed, you can switch the left and right button configuration. You can increase or decrease the speed, or sensitivity, with which the pointer responds to mouse movements. You can also adjust how fast or slow your double-click action can be. You can change your mouse device driver. You can even change the graphics for your mouse pointers.

Change your mouse pointer speed

Perhaps your mouse pointer seems slow to you and you want to speed it up to make it more responsive to your slightest movement. In this exercise, you'll use the Mouse Properties dialog box to increase the mouse pointer speed.

Mouse

1   With the Control Panel still open, double-click the Mouse icon.

The Mouse Properties dialog box appears.

2   Click the Motion tab.

The Motion tab appears.

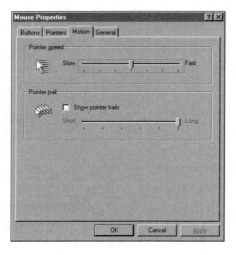

3 Drag the Pointer Speed slider a little to the right to make the mouse pointer a little faster, and then click Apply.

As you move your mouse around the screen, you should already notice a difference in the mouse pointer response. Make any further adjustments if you want.

4 Click OK.

Change the mouse button setup

Perhaps you're left-handed and you want to change the primary button to the right button, and the secondary button to the left button. In this exercise, you'll change your mouse button setup.

NOTE If you like your mouse button configuration the way it is, you can skip this exercise, or you can experiment with this exercise and then change it back to your original setup.

1 In the Control Panel window, double-click the Mouse icon.

2 In the Mouse Properties dialog box, be sure that the Buttons tab is active.

3 Click the Left-Handed option button.

4 Click OK.

The mouse is reconfigured to a left-handed setup. The right mouse button is now the primary button.

5 Click the Close button on the Control Panel window.

6 Unless you prefer a left-handed button configuration, change the button configuration back to its original setting.

Remember, you'll have to use the right mouse button to open and make selections in the Mouse Properties dialog box.

Finish the lesson

1 Close all open windows by clicking the Close button in the upper-right corner of each window.

2 If any window is minimized, use the right mouse button to click the window's taskbar button, and then click Close.

You are now ready to start the next lesson, or you can work on your own.

3 If you are finished using Windows 95 for now, on the Start menu click Shut Down, and then click Yes.

Lesson Summary

To	Do this
Open the Taskbar Properties dialog box	Use the right mouse button to click an empty area on the taskbar, and then click Properties.
Add a command to the Start menu or Programs menu	Open the Taskbar Properties dialog box. On the Start Menu Programs tab, click Add. Type the name of the program in the Command Line text box, and then click Next. Click the Start Menu or Programs folder, and then click Next. Type the name you want the shortcut command to have, and then click Finish. Click OK.
Remove a command from the Start menu or Programs menu	Open the Taskbar Properties dialog box. On the Start Menu Programs tab, click Remove. In the next window, click the item to remove, and then click Remove. Click Close, and then click OK on the tab.
Add a shortcut icon to the Desktop	Find where the item is stored on your hard disk. Use the right mouse button to drag the item to the Desktop, and then click Create Shortcut(s) Here.

To	Do this
Rename a shortcut icon	Use the right mouse button to click the shortcut icon. On the pop-up menu, click Rename. Type the new name, and then press ENTER.
Remove a shortcut icon from the Desktop	Drag the icon to the Recycle Bin icon. *or* Use the right mouse button to click the icon, click Delete, and then click the Yes button.
Create a StartUp shortcut	Open the Taskbar Properties dialog box. On the Start Menu Programs tab, click Add. In the dialog box, click Browse. Find and then double-click the program you want. Click Next. In the dialog box, click the StartUp folder. Click Next, and then click Finish. In the dialog box, click OK.
Remove a StartUp shortcut	Open the Taskbar Properties dialog box. On the Start Menu Programs tab, click Remove. In the dialog box, double-click the StartUp folder, click the shortcut to remove, and then click Remove. Click close and then click OK.
Open Control Panel	Click Start, point to Settings, and then click Control Panel. *or* Double-click My Computer, and then double-click the Control Panel folder.
Customize your display, including the background, screen saver, and colors	Use the right mouse button to click the Desktop, and then click Properties. In the Display Properties dialog box, click the appropriate tab and then select the settings you want.
Customize your mouse	In Control Panel, double-click the Mouse icon. In the Mouse Properties dialog box, click the appropriate tab, and then select the settings you want.

For online information about	From the Help dialog box, click Index and then type
Customizing your Start menu and Programs menu	**customizing, the Start menu**
Creating and using shortcuts	**shortcuts**
Customizing the Windows 95 setup with Control Panel	**Control Panel**

For more information on	In *Introducing Microsoft Windows 95*, see
Customizing your Start menu and Programs menu	Chapter 2, "Beyond the Basics"
Creating and using shortcuts	Chapter 2, "Beyond the Basics"
Customizing your Windows 95 setup with Control Panel	Chapter 1, "The Basics"

Preview of the Next Lessons

In Part 2, "Doing Your Work with Windows 95," you'll use Windows 95 to work with programs that help you do your day-to-day work. You'll learn how Windows-based programs operate, and you'll see how MS-DOS–based programs run under Windows 95. In Lesson 3, "Using Windows 95 Accessories," you'll use WordPad and Paint, already introduced in Part 1.

Review & Practice

In the lessons in Part 1, "Going to Work with Windows 95," you learned skills to help you use different windows, navigate within file structures, and customize your Desktop. If you want to practice these skills and test your understanding before you proceed with the lessons in Part 2, you can work through the Review & Practice section following this lesson.

Review & Practice

You will review and practice how to:

Estimated time
25 min.

- Locate files, start programs, and open documents.
- Manage open items with the taskbar.
- Look up information in the online Help system.
- Add and remove commands on your Start and Programs menus.
- Create shortcuts on your Desktop.

Before you go on to Part 2, you can practice the navigation and customization skills you learned in Part 1 by working through the steps in this Review & Practice section.

Scenario

You have just started working for Childs Play, Inc., and you have acquired your new computer, complete with Microsoft Windows 95. You have used Microsoft Windows 3.1 in the past, and you want to explore how to get around in Windows 95. You also want to customize Windows 95 to the way you like to work.

Step 1:   Start Programs and Open Documents

In this step, you'll find the files, start the programs, and open the documents with which you want to work.

Start programs from the Start menu

➤ With Windows 95 running, use the Start button to start WordPad, Paint, and Windows Explorer.

Open documents

1 Use Windows Explorer to open the History document, which is in your Windows 95 Practice folder.

2 Open My Computer, and browse through the appropriate disks and folders to find and open the Logo Yellows document, which is also in your Windows 95 Practice folder.

For more information on	See
Starting programs in Windows 95	Lesson 1
Finding documents in Windows 95	Lesson 1

Step 2: Manage Open Items with the Taskbar

Your Desktop now has several overlapping windows. In this step, you'll organize your Desktop, but you'll still keep your programs and documents open so that you can get to them quickly.

Minimize and restore windows

1 Bring the Windows Explorer window to the top of the stack of windows. (Hint: On the taskbar, click Exploring.)

2 Minimize Windows Explorer.

3 Bring the History document to the top of the stack of windows.

4 Minimize the History window.

5 Minimize the Logo Yellows window.

6 Restore the Logo Yellows window.

7 Minimize the Windows 95 Practice folder window.

Hide and show the taskbar

1 Hide the taskbar. (Hint: Use the right mouse button to click an empty area of the taskbar, then click Properties.)

2 Temporarily display the taskbar. (Hint: Move your mouse pointer to the last location of the taskbar.)

3 Permanently display the taskbar.

Move and resize the taskbar

1 Move the taskbar to the right edge of your Desktop.
2 Widen the taskbar so that you see more of the names on the taskbar.
3 Move the taskbar to the top of your Desktop.
4 Widen the taskbar so that it displays two rows of buttons.
5 Move the taskbar back to its original position at the bottom of your Desktop.

Close all open windows

1 Close all open windows appearing on the Desktop.
2 Close any items that are minimized on the taskbar without opening them first. (Hint: Use the right mouse button to click the item name on the taskbar.)

For more information on	See
Managing your windows	Lesson 1

Step 3: Look Up Information in Online Help

Because you're new to Windows 95, you rely on the online Help system to answer questions that arise as you work. In this step, you'll look up information on how to customize your taskbar. You'll also look up information about changing your screen saver and managing your open windows.

Find help for a general category

1 Use the Start button to start the online Help system.
2 On the Contents tab, expand the topic "Introducing Windows."
3 Expand the Help topic "Tips and Tricks."
4 Expand the Help topic "For Setting Up the Desktop Efficiently."
5 Read the Help topic "Customizing the taskbar."
6 Close the open Help topic.

Find help for a specific topic

1 In the online Help system, use the Index to search for "display."
2 Read the Help topic "protecting by using a screen saver."
3 Return to the Index, and search for "window." (Hint: Click the Help Topics button in the topics window.)
4 Read the Help topic "tiling windows."
5 Close the open Help topic window.

For more information on	See
Getting Help with Windows 95	Lesson 1

Step 4: Customize Your Menus

As you continue to use Windows 95, you recognize which programs and utilities you tend to use most often. In this step, you'll add the commands for two programs you use every day to your Start menu. You'll also add the commands for other programs to your Programs menu to help make your work more efficient.

1   Add WordPad to your Start menu. (Hint: Use the right mouse button to click the taskbar, and then click Properties.)

2   Use your new Start menu to start WordPad.

3   Add Paint to your Programs menu. (Hint: In the Command Line text box, type **mspaint**.)

4   Use your new Programs menu to start Paint.

5   Close WordPad and Paint.

For more information on	See
Customizing your menus	Lesson 2

Step 5: Create Shortcut Icons on Your Desktop

There is a program, a folder, and a document that you use nearly every day. In this step, you'll create shortcuts to these items so that you don't lose any time browsing through the system to find them.

Add shortcuts to your Desktop

1   Find where the Calculator accessory is stored on your computer system. (Hint: On the Start menu, point to Find, and then click Files Or Folders. The file is called "Calc.")

2   Create a shortcut to Calculator on your Desktop. (Hint: Use the right mouse button to drag.)

3   Rename this shortcut **Calculator**

4   Use Windows Explorer to find the Letters folder in your Windows 95 Practice folder.

5   Create a shortcut to the Letters folder on your Desktop.

6   Rename this shortcut **Letters & Memos**

7   Open My Computer, and find the Dept Logo Color file within another folder in the Windows 95 Practice folder.

8   Create a shortcut to this file on your Desktop.

9   Rename this shortcut **Dept Logo**

Use your shortcuts

1   Close any open windows on your Desktop.

2   Double-click the Calculator shortcut to start it.

3   Double-click the Letters & Memos shortcut to open it.

4   Double-click the Dept Logo shortcut to open it in Paint.

5   Close all open windows.

For more information on	See
Creating shortcuts	Lesson 2

Step 6:   Reset Your Windows 95 Setup

In this step, you'll reverse the changes you've made in this Review & Practice section so that your Windows 95 setup is the same as when you started. This way, your screen setup will match the illustrations in the following lessons.

Remove commands from your Start and Programs menus

1   Remove the WordPad command from your Start menu. (Hint: Use the right mouse button to click the taskbar, and then click Properties.)

2   Remove the Paint command from your Programs menu.

Remove shortcuts from your Desktop

1   Remove one of your shortcuts from your Desktop with the Delete command. (Hint: Use the right mouse button to click the icon.)

2   Remove the other two shortcuts from your Desktop by using Recycle Bin.

For more information on	See
Customizing your menus	Lesson 2
Creating shortcuts	Lesson 2

Finish the Review & Practice

1   Close all open windows by clicking the Close button in the upper-right corner of each window.

2   If any window is minimized, use the right mouse button to click the window's taskbar button, and then click Close.

You are now ready to start the next lesson, or you can work on your own.

3   If you are finished using Windows 95 for now, on the Start menu click Shut Down, and then click Yes.

Doing Your Work with Windows 95

Part 2

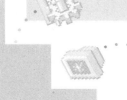

Using Windows 95 Accessories

Estimated time
40 min.

In this lesson you will learn how to:

- Locate, start, and use accessories in Windows 95.
- Create, edit, and format text documents using WordPad.
- Create, edit, and color drawings using Paint.

You probably wouldn't spend all your time at work wandering around the building or decorating your office. At some point, you need to get down to your actual work. In the same way, the purpose for using Microsoft Windows 95 is not to see what one icon does or to experiment with all the different screen savers available. The real reason you're using a computer in the first place is that you have actual work to do.

Windows 95 comes with several programs, called *accessories*, that you can use to do some of your work. In Microsoft Windows 3.1, you might have used accessories such as Write, Paintbrush, Notepad, Calendar, and Terminal. In Windows 95, you have accessories such as WordPad, Paint, HyperTerminal, and Fax Viewer. With accessories, you can type and print short documents, draw simple pictures, and connect to other computers. In this lesson, you'll first review the accessories in Windows 95. Then you'll use two of the most commonly used accessories to write a memo and to draw a picture.

Looking at Your Windows 95 Accessories

In your work area, you might keep various supplies, resources, and equipment handy to help you do your work. Your supplies might include a notepad and a briefcase. Your equipment might include your calculator, telephone, fax machine, and tape recorder.

In Windows 3.1, you might have used accessories to help you with your everyday work or to help you use your computer more efficiently. In Windows 95, you have an even greater variety of accessories that act as supplies, resources, and equipment. The Windows 95 Accessories menu looks like the following.

If your menu looks different from this illustration, refer to "Matching the Exercises" in the Appendix.

The following table lists the accessories by category, describes their functions and, where applicable, lists their equivalent functions in Windows 3.1. Some accessories require appropriate hardware to be available, such as a modem or CD-ROM device.

Desktop accessory	Function	Windows 3.1 accessory
Calculator	Displays a calculator that you can use to perform simple, scientific, and statistical calculations.	Calculator
Character Map	Displays special characters that you can insert into your documents.	Character Map
Clipboard Viewer	Displays the contents of your Clipboard, showing items you have cut or copied while you work in programs.	Clipboard
Notepad	Allows you to create or view short, unformatted text documents.	Notepad
Paint	Allows you to create, edit, or view pictures.	Paintbrush
WordPad	Allows you to create, edit, format, or view short documents.	Write

Telecommunication accessory		Function	Windows 3.1 accessory
	Dial-Up Networking	Uses modems and telephone lines to connect your computer to another computer that you call. You can share information between the two computers, even when you're not on a network. Both computers must be running Windows 95 or Microsoft Windows NT.	None
	Direct Cable Connection	Physically connects your computer to another computer with a cable. You can share information between the two computers, even when you're not on a network. Both computers must be running Windows 95.	None
	HyperTerminal (folder)	Connects to a remote computer using a modem. Sends and receives files, connects to online services, bulletin boards, and other information programs. Connects to computers running different operating systems. Any connections you set up are stored in the folder.	Terminal
	Phone Dialer	Places telephone calls from your computer, using your modem or another Windows telecommunication device.	Terminal

Fax accessory		Function	Windows 3.1 accessory
	Compose New Fax	Displays an editing screen in which you can write a fax message.	None
	Cover Page Editor	Allows you to write a cover page for a file to be faxed.	None
	Retrieve File	Displays fax files received on your computer.	None

Multimedia accessory	Function	Windows 3.1 accessory
CD Player	Plays audio compact discs from a CD-ROM drive connected to your computer.	None
Media Player	Plays audio, video, or animation files. Controls multimedia hardware devices. This is available if your hardware setup includes a sound card.	Media Player
Sound Recorder	Allows you to create, play back, edit, and insert sound clips into documents.	Sound Recorder
Volume Control	Controls the volume and balance of your sound card.	None

System accessory	Function	Windows 3.1 accessory
Backup	Copies files from the hard disk to floppy disks, tape, or another computer on the network to back up your files. Restores back-up files.	File Manager
Disk Defragmenter	Optimizes your disk so that files and unused space are used efficiently.	None
DriveSpace	Compresses data on hard and floppy disks, creating more free space.	None
Net Watcher	Lists the names of users who are currently using resources on your computer and who have used them in the past. Manages shared folders to your computer. Disconnects users from your computer.	None
Scan Disk	Checks a disk for logical or physical problems, and then marks the bad areas so that data is not written to those areas.	None

System accessory		Function	Windows 3.1 accessory
	System Monitor	Shows a graph that reflects the current, real-time use and activity of your computer's internal core processor (central processing unit).	None

Games accessory		Function	Windows 3.1 accessory
	FreeCell	Displays a solitaire card game.	None
	Hearts	Displays a group or solitaire card game.	None
	Minesweeper	Displays a strategy board game.	Minesweeper
	Party Line	Displays a network "party line" game.	None
	Solitaire	Displays a solitaire card game.	Solitaire

The following illustration shows a few Windows 95 accessories open on the Desktop.

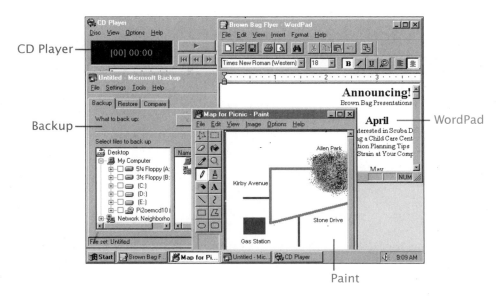

CD Player

Backup

WordPad

Paint

Writing with WordPad

In a typical workday, you might need to write one or more documents, such as a memo, letter, or report. Although you could use a full-featured word processing program, such as Microsoft Word, to do these tasks, WordPad is useful for small, simpler documents. In Windows 3.1, Write was the accessory that served this function, but it had limited formatting capabilities. With WordPad, you can create, edit, and format a new document. You can also print the document and save it for later use.

Each time you start WordPad, you see a blank WordPad screen. This is like a blank sheet of paper on which you can write your document. When you are ready to write, simply begin typing. As you reach the end of a line, WordPad automatically breaks the line near the right margin and moves the last word to the next line as you continue typing. This feature is called *wordwrap*. You do not have to press ENTER (comparable to the carriage return key on a typewriter) to go to the next line, unless you are ending a paragraph or typing short lines.

Create a new document in WordPad

Suppose you want to write a memo to all employees that announces the company picnic. In this exercise, you'll use WordPad to write and save the memo.

If your computer isn't already on, turn it on now. If you see the Welcome dialog box, click the Close button.

1   Click Start. On the Start menu, point to Programs, and then point to Accessories.

2   On the Accessories menu, click WordPad.

WordPad starts. As in other Windows applications you might have used, at the top of the window are the menu bar, the Standard toolbar, and the format bar.

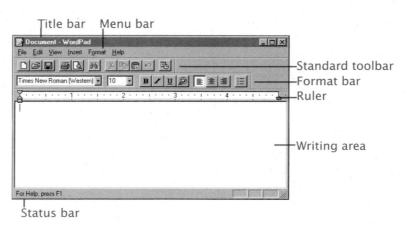

3   Click the Maximize button on the WordPad window, if it is not already maximized.

4 In the writing area of the WordPad window, type the following:

TO: All Employees

FROM: Childs Play Management

This month marks our 15th year of business. We will be celebrating this event with a company picnic on Friday, June 9. The picnic begins at 10:00 AM, and everyone is invited to join the fun. See you there!

If your memo did not wordwrap, click Options on the View menu. In the Word Wrap box, click Wrap To Ruler, and then click OK.

Save

5 On the Standard toolbar, click the Save button to display the Save As dialog box.

6 Below the Save In list box, double-click My Computer, and then double-click the hard disk (C:).

The folders stored on your hard disk appear in the list box.

7 Double-click the Windows 95 Practice folder. Use the scroll bar if necessary.

In Windows 95, you are no longer restricted to an eight-letter maximum filename with a three-letter maximum extension. In Windows 95, you can now make your filename as long as you want it to be (up to 255 characters). You can also use spaces in the filename.

8 Double-click the File Name text box, type **Picnic Memo.wri** and then click Save.

The file is saved in your Windows 95 Practice folder, and the name Picnic Memo appears in the WordPad title bar and on the taskbar.

9 Click the Close button to close the WordPad window.

The WordPad window containing the memo closes.

Retrieve a WordPad document

A day or two has passed since you created the Picnic Memo. You want to retrieve and then edit the memo. In this exercise, you open the memo.

1 Click Start. On the Start menu, point to Programs, and then point to Accessories.

2 On the Accessories menu, click WordPad to start it.

Open

3 On the Standard toolbar in WordPad, click the Open button.

The Open dialog box appears.

4 Below the Look In list box, double-click My Computer, and then double-click the hard disk (C:).

The contents of your hard disk appear.

5 Double-click the Windows 95 Practice folder. Use your scroll bar if necessary.

6 In the Files Of Type list box, click the down arrow and then click All Documents.

All files stored in the Windows 95 Practice folder appear. The files are listed in alphabetical order.

7 Double-click the Picnic Memo file.

You might need to use your scroll bar to locate the file. Your memo opens in the WordPad window.

 TIP You can also open a document on which you have recently worked by using the Documents menu. To do this, click Start. On the Start menu, point to Documents. The Documents menu lists up to the last 15 documents you have opened in any program. Click the document, and it opens in the program with which it was created.

Edit your WordPad document

You need to change the date and some wording in your memo. In this exercise, you insert, replace, and delete words and characters to make necessary editing changes.

1 Maximize the Picnic Memo window, if it is not already maximized.

2 Click just before the "j" in "join the fun," and then type the following:

take a paid vacation day off and

Your new text appears before the text already in place. The sentence now reads "The picnic begins at 10:00 AM, and everyone is invited to take a paid vacation day off and join the fun."

3   Select the text "June 9," and then type **July 14**

"July 14" replaces "June 9."

4   Double-click the word "vacation," and then press DELETE or BACKSPACE.

The word "vacation" is deleted.

5   Move "See you there" to a second paragraph by clicking just before the "S" in "See you there," and then pressing ENTER twice.

6   With your pointer already before the "S" in "See you there," press TAB.

The line is indented one-half inch.

7   Click just before the "T" in "This month marks..." in the first paragraph. Be sure that you have not highlighted any text and that you see the blinking insertion point. Press TAB.

Your memo should look similar to the following illustration.

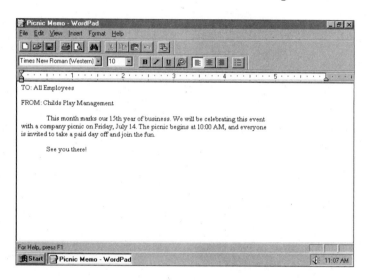

8   On the Standard toolbar, click the Save button.

Save

If you do not see the format bar on your screen, on the View menu, click Format Bar.

Change the font

Now that the words of your memo are exactly as you want them, you want to format the memo to make it look more polished. In this exercise, you use the format bar, shown in the following illustration, to change the font throughout the document.

1   On the Edit menu in WordPad, click Select All.

Your entire document is selected.

2   On the format bar, open the Font list box by clicking its down arrow.

Times New Roman (Western) ▾ ◀—Click here.

3   In the Font list box, click Arial.

If you do not have the Arial font set up on your computer, choose any other font you want. The new font you specified is applied to all the text in your memo.

4   On the format bar, click the down arrow next to the Font Size list box, and then click 14.

The new font size is applied to all the text in your memo.

Italic

5   Select the words "paid day off," and then on the format bar, click the Italic button.

The selected words are changed to italic type.

6   Select the "TO:" and "FROM:" memo header lines.

Bold

7   In the format bar, click the Bold button.

Your memo should look similar to the following illustration.

You can also use the format bar to change the justification of paragraphs in your document.

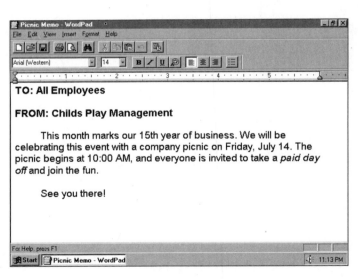

8   On the Standard toolbar, click the Save button.

Save

TIP   You can also use the Font command on the Format menu to make these and other font changes to your document.

Preview the memo

In this exercise, you view the memo to see how it will look when you print it.

Print Preview

You can also choose Print Preview from the File menu.

NOTE   You must have a printer driver installed to use Print Preview and to use all the features in Page Setup.

1   On the Standard toolbar, click the Print Preview button.

The Print Preview screen appears, showing a picture of the page on which the memo is typed, including the margin settings and any other page settings you have specified.

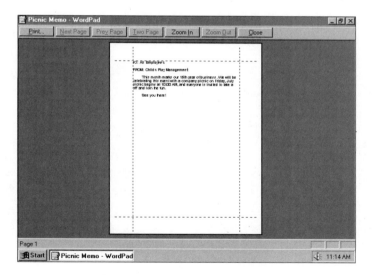

2   On the Print Preview toolbar, click Close.

The Print Preview screen closes, and the WordPad editing screen appears again.

Set the margins

As a finishing touch to your memo, you want to widen your margins. In this exercise, you change your margin settings.

1   On the File menu in WordPad, click Page Setup.

The Page Setup dialog box appears.

2   In the Margins area, double-click the Left text box to select the text, and then type **2** to indicate a two-inch left margin.

The sample document reflects your change.

3   Double-click the Right text box, and type **1.5** to specify the size of the right margin.

The default unit of measurement is inches.

4   Click OK.

The margins of your memo change according to your specifications, although you might not immediately see the difference on the screen.

Print Preview

5   On the Standard toolbar, click the Print Preview button.

The Print Preview screen appears, showing your new margin settings.

6   Click Close.

The Print Preview screen closes, and the WordPad editing screen appears again.

7   On the Standard toolbar, click the Save button.

Save

Print your memo

You have finished the memo, you've previewed it, and you're now ready to print it for distribution. In this exercise, you'll print the document.

   NOTE   If your computer is not connected to a printer, skip this exercise. For more information about installing a printer with Windows 95, refer to "Changing Your Setup" in the Appendix.

1 Turn on the printer that is connected to your computer.

2 On the Standard toolbar, click the Print button.

Print

Your memo is printed on your printer, using the standard default printer settings from the Print dialog box.

3 Click the Restore button on the WordPad window to restore the window to its previous size.

4 Close all open windows.

 TIP You can also use the Print command on the File menu to change your print options and to print a document.

Drawing Pictures with Paint

Another activity in a typical workday might be to create a simple drawing to accompany or complement a text document. In Windows 3.1, you could do this with the Paintbrush accessory. In Windows 95, you can draw simple pictures, logos, maps, and symbols with the Paint accessory, which has many of the same features as Paintbrush. With Paint, you can create, edit, move, and size a drawing. You can also print the drawing and save it on your disk for later use.

In Paint, you can use the *toolbox*, which contains tools for creating shapes, lines, and other drawing elements. There is also a color box from which you can select the line and fill colors for your drawing elements.

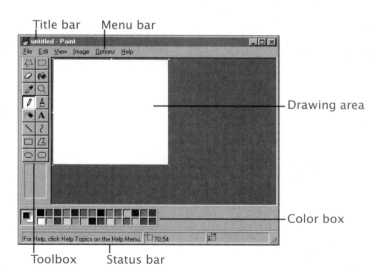

The toolbox includes drawing tools you can use to draw shapes, color areas, select shapes, add text, edit lines, and more. The following illustration shows the names of all the drawing tools available on the toolbox.

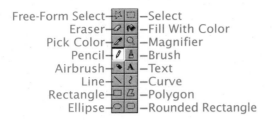

Suppose you are working on a product logo concept for Childs Play's new preschool product line. In the following exercises, you'll use Paint to create a drawing for this product line. When you're finished, your logo will look similar to the following illustration.

Set the drawing size

In this exercise, you'll start Paint and set the drawing size—the first steps in creating your new logo.

1   Click Start. On the Start menu, point to Programs, and then point to Accessories.

2   On the Accessories menu, click Paint.

Paint starts.

3   Maximize the Paint window by clicking the Maximize button.

4   On the Image menu, click Attributes.

The Attributes dialog box appears. The width and height are currently expressed in *pixels*, or *pels*. Pixels are "picture elements," the smallest graphic unit that can be displayed on your screen. Pixels make up all the shapes you see on your screen, whether they are fonts, lines, or circles. By using different colors for certain pixels, such as black or white, you can see the pixels form different shapes.

5 In the Units area, click Inches.

The width and height change to inches.

6 Double-click the number in the Width text box, and then type **4**

7 Press TAB, and then in the Height text box, type **3**

8 Click OK.

The drawing area changes to 4x3 inches.

Draw, select, and copy shapes

In this exercise, you'll use the Rectangle tool to begin drawing your logo. You'll also use the Select tool to select graphic objects you want to edit. You'll use the Copy and Paste commands to duplicate graphic objects in your drawing.

Rectangle

1 In the toolbox, click the Rectangle tool.

2 Hold down SHIFT and then, in the upper-left corner of your drawing area, drag from the upper-left corner toward the lower-right corner to draw a square. Referring to the status area in the lower-right corner of the Paint window, make your square approximately 100x100 pixels.

Holding down SHIFT ensures that you drag a perfect square, rather than a rectangle. The size of any shape you draw appears in the status area, as measured in pixels.

Select

3 Click the Select tool.

Wherever you drag, a dotted line will appear. You can use this *selection box* to specify the graphic objects you want to select for further editing.

4 Drag a selection box around your square.

This selects your square so that you can copy it.

5 On the Edit menu, click Copy.

Nothing appears to change on the computer screen. But the square, which is contained within the selection, is copied into the computer's memory.

6 On the Edit menu, click Paste.

The contents of your copied selection appear in the upper-left corner of your drawing area.

7 Drag the pasted square in front of your original square, as shown in the following illustration.

Opaque

8 Below the toolbox, click the Opaque option, which is the first of the two options displayed, Opaque and Transparent.

9 Click anywhere in the drawing area to permanently place the top square.

The top square covers some of the lines of the second square, similar to the following illustration.

Draw lines and save the graphics file

In this exercise, you'll use the Line tool to connect the two squares. You'll also name and save the Paint file in your Windows 95 Practice folder.

Line

1 Click the Line tool.

2 In your drawing area, drag from the upper-left corner of one square to the upper-left corner of the other square. Use the crosshair mouse pointer to help you position the line precisely.

A line connects the two rectangles.

3 Drag a line between the two upper-right corners of the squares.

4 Drag a line between the two lower-left corners of the squares.

The squares are connected, creating a cube, as shown in the following illustration.

Save

5 On the File menu, click Save.

The Save As dialog box appears.

6 Below the Save In list box, double-click My Computer, and then double-click the hard disk (C:).

7 Double-click the Windows 95 Practice folder. Use the scroll bar if necessary.

8 Double-click the File Name text box, type **Preschool Toys Logo**, and then click Save.

The file is saved in your Windows 95 Practice folder.

Zoom and edit the drawing

Suppose you want to make your drawing look more like a block. In this exercise, you'll erase extra lines from the block.

Magnifier

Eraser

1 Click the Magnifier tool.

2 In the drawing area, click the magnifier tool over the lower-left corner of the cube.

The part of the drawing that you clicked is magnified.

3 Click the Eraser tool.

4 Drag the Eraser tool over the extra horizontal line of the back square of the block.

The line is erased. If you accidentally erase too much, on the Edit menu, click Undo, and then try again.

5 Click the Magnifier tool again, and then click anywhere in the drawing area.

The drawing returns to its original size.

If you want a greater magnification, click Custom on the View menu, and then choose the magnification you want.

6 Click the Magnifier tool, and then click the upper-right corner of the block.

The part of the drawing that you clicked is magnified.

7 Drag the Eraser tool over the extra vertical line of the back square until it is erased.

8 Click the Magnifier tool, and then click anywhere in the drawing area.

The drawing returns to its original size. Your block should look similar to the following illustration.

9 On the File menu, click Save.

Add text to the drawing

In this exercise, you'll add the block alphabet letters and the logo text. When your logo is finished, it will look similar to the following illustration.

Text

1   Click the Text tool.

2   In the drawing, drag a square inside the top center of the block.

An insertion point appears in the text entry area, and the Text toolbar appears at the top of the window. If you don't see the toolbar, open the View menu and click Text Toolbar.

3   In the text entry area, type **A**

4   In the text toolbar, select the Arial font, 14 point size, Bold, and Italic.

The text reflects your changes.

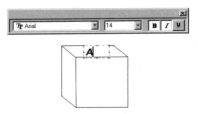

Transparent

5   Below the toolbox, click the Transparent option, which is the second of the two options, Opaque and Transparent.

6   If the "A" is not positioned where you want, click the Select tool, draw a selection box around the "A," being careful not to select any part of the block itself, and then drag to move the letter where you want it.

7   Follow the same procedure to type **B** on the left side of the block.

8   On the front of the block, use the Text tool and type **Childs Play** in 10-point Arial bold italic.

9   Click the Text tool again, and type **Kid Stuff** in 16-point Arial bold.

Draw a circle

In this exercise, you'll use the Ellipse tool to draw a circle around the cube.

Ellipse

1   Click the Ellipse tool.

2 Hold down SHIFT and then drag from above the upper-left corner of the cube to beyond the lower-right corner of the cube to draw a circle.

Holding down SHIFT ensures that you drag a perfect circle.

3 From the File menu, click Save.

Add color to your drawing

You can add colors to your drawing. This can be especially useful if you use a color printer. If you're using a black-and-white printer, the colors appear on your screen and are reproduced in different shades of gray on your printed page. In this exercise, you'll fill different parts of the drawing with color.

1 On the color box, click any shade of green you want.

2 Click the Fill With Color tool.

Fill With Color

3 Click the front of the block.

The front face of the block is filled with the color green.

4 Use this procedure to fill the areas of the drawing with the colors indicated in the following illustration.

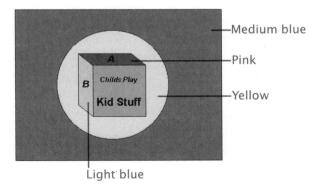

If a section of the drawing is filled with a color you did not want, this might mean that a graphic object is not completely enclosed. When there are open lines in a graphic object, the color "leaks" out to other objects. You can repair broken lines by connecting them with the Line or Curve tool.

5 From the File menu, click Save.

Print your drawing

You now want to print the drawing to have it reviewed by the Advertising Department. In this exercise, you'll view and print the drawing.

 NOTE If your computer is not connected to a printer, skip this exercise. For more information about installing a printer, refer to "Changing Your Setup" in the Appendix.

1 On the File menu, click Print Preview.

A drawing of a page appears with your logo in the upper-left corner.

2 On the Print Preview window, click Close.

3 Turn on the printer that is connected to your computer.

4 On the File menu, click Print.

The Print dialog box appears.

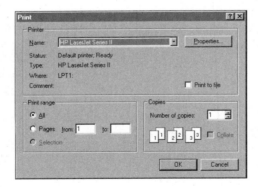

5 Click OK.

Your drawing is printed.

Restore

6 Restore the Paint window to its previous size by clicking the Restore button.

Finish the lesson

1   Close all open windows by clicking the Close button in the upper-right corner of each window.

2   If any window is minimized, use the right mouse button to click the window's taskbar button, and then click Close.

You are now ready to start the next lesson, or you can work on your own.

3   If you are finished using Windows 95 for now, on the Start menu click Shut Down, and then click Yes.

Lesson Summary

To	Do this	Button
Start and use Windows 95 accessories	On the Start menu, point to Programs, and then point to Accessories. Click the accessory you want to start.	
Change the text font in a WordPad document	In the WordPad document, select the text whose font you want to change. On the format bar, click the font, font size, or font style.	
Set the margins in a WordPad document	On the File menu, click Page Setup. In the Margins area, type the left, right, top, or bottom margins you want, and then click OK.	
Save a WordPad document	On the toolbar, click the Save button.	
Print a WordPad document	On the toolbar, click the Print button.	
Draw simple shapes	Click the tool for the shape you want to draw, and then drag the shape in the drawing area.	
Select a portion of your drawing	Click the Select tool.	
Zoom a portion of your drawing	Click the Magnifier tool.	
Erase a portion of your drawing	Click the Eraser tool.	
Add text to a drawing	Click the Text tool.	
Add color to a drawing	On the color box, click the color you want. Click the Fill With Color tool, and then click the area to fill.	

For online information about	From the Help dialog box, click Index and then type
Creating and editing text documents using WordPad	**WordPad**
Creating, editing, and viewing drawings using Paint	**Paint**
Opening and using the Windows 95 accessories	*the accessory name*

For more information on	In *Introducing Microsoft Windows 95*, see
Creating and editing text documents using WordPad	Chapter 3, "The Possibilities"
Creating, editing, and viewing drawings using Paint	Chapter 3, "The Possibilities"
Opening and using the Windows 95 accessories	Chapter 3, "The Possibilities"

Preview of the Next Lesson

In Lesson 4, "Working with Your Programs," you'll learn how to use Windows-based programs that you set up to work with Windows 95, and you'll learn about sharing information between different programs. You'll also learn how to use MS-DOS–based programs with Windows 95. You'll use an MS-DOS window with a toolbar, and you'll start and stop MS-DOS–based programs.

Working with Your Programs

Estimated time
40 min.

In this lesson you will learn how to:

- Browse for and run Windows-based programs.
- Run and switch among a variety of open programs.
- Share information between different programs.
- Use MS-DOS–based programs.

When you need specialized programs to do specific types of work, you set up and use programs beyond those that come with Microsoft Windows 95. You might do your everyday work on the computer by using a spreadsheet, database, project management, or page layout program. While the majority of these programs are probably designed to run on Windows 95 as *Windows–based programs*, you might also have programs that run on MS-DOS. Although Windows 95 replaces MS-DOS as an operating system, you can still run your *MS-DOS–based programs*. With Windows 95, you'll find that switching between and sharing information among multiple programs is even easier than with Microsoft Windows 3.1.

Working with Windows-Based Programs

In Windows 3.1, you might have had a program group in Program Manager called "applications" that included programs you acquired separately, developed by Microsoft or other software developers. Examples of such programs are Microsoft Access, WordPerfect for Windows, Microsoft PowerPoint, and Aldus PageMaker. Regardless of the type of program you have, or who developed it, all Windows-based programs have certain elements in common, and you can count on these characteristics as you move from one Windows-based program to another. The following illustration shows a few Windows-based programs open on the Desktop.

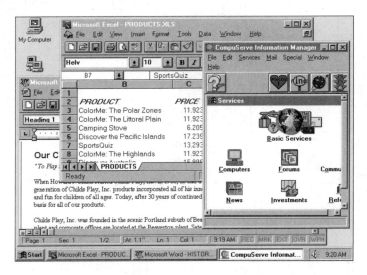

When a Windows-based program opens in a window, you see the familiar window controls, including the Minimize, Maximize, and Close buttons. If the window's contents extend beyond its boundaries, you'll also see the horizontal and vertical scroll bars.

Each Windows-based program has a menu bar, across the top of its window, from which you can choose commands to control the program. Many programs also use one or more toolbars, on which you can click a button that acts as a command shortcut.

In previous lessons, you used Windows 95 accessories, the programs that come with Windows 95. You found that to start any accessory, you open the Accessories menu, and then click the accessory name. To start a Windows-based program, you browse through My Computer or Windows Explorer to find the program file and then double-click the filename. If you prefer to start the program by clicking an icon or a command, you can create a shortcut to the program on the Start menu, the Programs menu, or the Desktop.

Browse for and run a Windows-based program

To set up a new program on your computer, see "Preparing to Use Windows 95" in the Appendix.

Suppose you have set up a new software program on your computer's hard disk and now you want to run it. In this exercise, you'll browse through your files to find and start a Windows-based program.

1   If your computer isn't already on, turn it on now. If you see the Welcome dialog box, click the Close button.

2   Double-click the My Computer icon.

3 Double-click the hard disk (C:) icon.

4 Double-click the Windows 95 Practice folder.

5 Double-click the Quotes folder.

The Quotes folder contains a program named "Quotables," along with a text file.

Quotables

6 Double-click the Quotables program file icon.

The Quotables program starts and displays the text of a famous quote. Although the quote might be different from the one shown here, your screen should look similar to the following illustration.

If your screen looks different from this illustration, refer to the "Matching the Exercises" section in the Appendix.

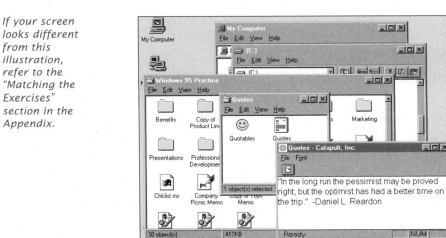

Next Quote

7 Click the Next Quote button.

The next quote appears.

8 Click the Close button to close the window and end the Quotables program.

> **TIP** If you don't know the name or general location of the program you want to run, you can use the Find command on the Start menu. Type any part of the program name you do know. Or, in the Find dialog box, click the Advanced tab, and click Applications. All programs with the parameters you entered will be found. You can double-click the program name to start it.

Create a shortcut to a Windows-based program

Let's say you use the Quotables program frequently. In this exercise, you'll make the Quotables program more readily available by creating a shortcut to it on your Desktop.

1 With the Quotes folder still open, use the right mouse button to drag the Quotables program file to any empty area on your Desktop.

A pop-up menu appears.

2 Click Create Shortcut Here.

An icon named "Shortcut To Quotables" appears on your Desktop.

3 Close all open windows.

Switching Among Multiple Open Programs

When working at a desk, you often have several documents or project folders available at one time. While you might be actively using one project folder, you know you can reach for and refer to another folder right there on your desk.

In the same way, you can use Windows 95 to keep several programs open at the same time, each one running in its own window on your Desktop. While one window is always active and visible on top of the other windows, you can quickly switch between and work in any of the other windows.

Suppose you've just created a drawing in Paint and you need to write a memo to accompany the drawing. While writing your memo, you find you need to make some calculations. In the following exercises, you'll switch among Paint, WordPad, and Calculator by using the taskbar and the keyboard.

Switch between Paint and WordPad using the taskbar

In this exercise, you'll write a memo to accompany your drawing.

1 Click Start. Point to Programs, point to Accessories, and then click Paint.

Paint starts.

2 On the File menu, click Open.

The Open dialog box appears.

3 Below the Look In list box, double-click My Computer, and then double-click the hard disk (C:).

The contents of your hard disk appear.

4 Double-click the Windows 95 Practice folder.

You might need to scroll to find it. The contents of the Windows 95 Practice folder appear.

5 Double-click Toys Logo to open the graphic in the Paint window.

6 Click Start again. Point to Programs, point to Accessories, and then click WordPad.

WordPad starts.

7 In WordPad, type the following note:

TO: Gwen Lehua, Advertising

FROM: Craig Armand, Marketing

Attached is a logo concept I sketched for our new preschool product line. Please develop the logo based on these ideas. Note that we are working on a budget of

You now need to make a calculation of your budget.

Switch between Calculator and WordPad

In this exercise, you'll switch between WordPad and Calculator to compute numbers you need in your WordPad memo.

1 Click Start. Point to Programs, point to Accessories, and then click Calculator.

Calculator starts.

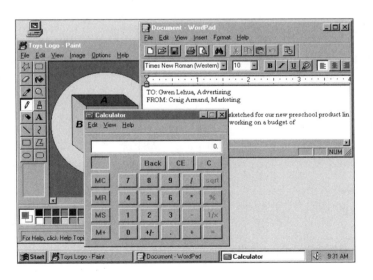

2 Use Calculator to figure 15% of 3500. Do this by typing the numbers and operators with the numeric keypad on your keyboard or by clicking the numbers and operators with your mouse on Calculator. Enter the formula as **3500 * 15%** using the Percent (%) function on Calculator.

Your result should be 525.

3 On the taskbar, click Document - WordPad.

WordPad becomes the active window.

4 Finish typing your memo where you left off, as follows:

$525.00 for this task. Let's meet next Tuesday to discuss this project in more detail. Thank you!

Save

5 On the Standard toolbar in WordPad, click the Save button.

The Save dialog box appears. Be sure that you're saving the memo on the hard disk (C:) in the Windows 95 Practice folder.

6 Double-click the File Name box, type **Preschool Toys Memo.wri**, and then click Save.

Switch between programs using the keyboard

Just as you can switch to a different program by clicking its name on the taskbar, you can switch between programs using the keyboard. In this exercise, you'll switch among Paint, WordPad, and Calculator by using the keyboard.

1 With the WordPad window still active, hold down ALT and press TAB. Do not release ALT yet.

A dialog box appears in the center of the screen, with icons that represent each of your open windows. The selected window is named at the bottom of the dialog box, and its icon is highlighted.

2 Continue to hold down the ALT key and press TAB repeatedly until the Paint icon is highlighted, and then release the ALT key.

Now Paint is the active window.

TIP Pressing ALT+ESC switches among items listed on the taskbar in sequence. If the window is currently open, it comes to the top of the Desktop. If the window is minimized, you can select it with ALT+ESC and then press ENTER to restore its window on the Desktop.

Arrange windows on the Desktop

Perhaps you want the WordPad and Calculator windows visible at the same time on your screen. In this exercise, you'll arrange, or *tile*, the two windows side by side. You'll also arrange your windows in a cascading fashion across the Desktop.

1 Minimize the Paint window.

2 Minimize any other windows that might be open on the Desktop except the WordPad and Calculator windows.

3 Use the right mouse button to click an empty space on the taskbar.

A pop-up menu appears, listing commands for arranging the open windows on the Desktop.

4 On the menu, click Tile Vertically.

The two open windows are arranged side by side on your Desktop.

If you want to restore your tiled windows to their previous sizes and shapes, use the right mouse button to click an empty space on the taskbar, and then click Undo Tile.

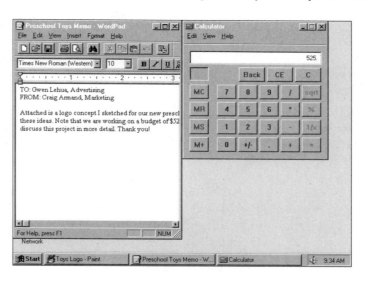

5 On the taskbar, click the Toys Logo - Paint button.

The Paint window appears on the Desktop.

6 Use the right mouse button to click an empty space on the taskbar.

7 On the pop-up menu, click Cascade.

The three open windows are arranged in a cascading fashion across your Desktop, and you can see the title bars of each window, as in the following illustration.

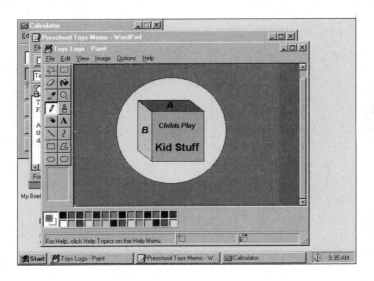

8   Close all open windows.

Sharing Information Between Different Programs

You have probably worked with paper documents in which one document had information you wanted to include in another document. To avoid the inconvenience of copying by hand, you might use scissors to cut information from one document and then use tape or paste to place that information in another document.

In Windows 95, as in Windows 3.1, you can electronically cut or copy information from one program and then paste the information into another program, for example, from Paint to WordPad, or from Microsoft Excel to Word.

In Windows 3.1, you might have taken this concept of sharing information several steps further, by *linking* information. Windows 95 continues this important capability. You can copy and paste information between applications so that the information is linked. Then, when the information changes in the original, or *source* document, it also changes automatically in the *destination* document.

And, just as in Windows 3.1, you can use Windows 95 to insert, or *embed*, a copy of a document from another program within your current program. With embedding, you can use the resources of another program without leaving your current program. This provides you with double the resources in just one document.

These capabilities are available in any Windows-based program—not just the programs and accessories that come with Windows 95—as long as the program has *OLE* capabilities. You know that your program has OLE linking capabilities if the program includes a command such as Paste Special or Paste Link, usually found on the Edit menu. You know that your program has OLE embedding capabilities if the program includes a command such as Insert Object, usually found on the Insert or Tools menu.

Find and open a Paint and a WordPad document

Imagine that you have used Paint to draw a map to the company picnic site. In this exercise, you'll open the map drawing in Paint and the picnic memo in WordPad. In a later exercise, you'll add the map to the memo.

1   Double-click the My Computer icon.

The My Computer window opens and displays the available disk drives on your computer.

2   Double-click the hard disk (C:) icon.

The (C:) window opens and displays the folders and files stored on the hard disk.

3   Double-click the Windows 95 Practice folder.

The Windows 95 Practice folder opens.

4   Double-click the Company Picnic Memo file.

The Company Picnic Memo file opens in a WordPad window.

5   On the taskbar, click the Windows 95 Practice folder button.

6   In the Windows 95 Practice folder, double-click the Map For Picnic file.

The Map For Picnic file opens in a Paint window.

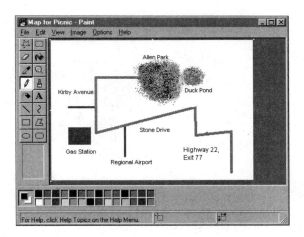

7   Maximize the Paint window.

Copy and paste from Paint to WordPad

In this exercise, you'll copy the map and paste it into your picnic memo.

Select

1   In Paint, click the Select tool.

2   Use the Select tool to drag a dotted rectangle around the entire map.

85

3 On the Edit menu in Paint, click Copy.

Although nothing appears to change on your screen, the map is temporarily copied into your computer memory.

4 On the taskbar, click Company Picnic Memo - WordPad.

The WordPad window appears.

5 Maximize the WordPad window.

6 Click at the end of the document, after "See you there!" Press ENTER twice to add two blank lines.

Paste

7 On the Standard toolbar in WordPad, click the Paste button.

The map drawing appears in your memo.

Save

8 On the Standard toolbar, click the Save button.

Print the document with the copied drawing

1 Be sure that your printer is on.

If you do not have an active printer that can print graphics, skip to step 3.

Print

2 On the Standard toolbar in WordPad, click the Print button.

The memo prints with the inserted map.

3 Close all open windows.

> **TIP** If you want to embed a copy of an object created in another program, first position your pointer where you want the embedded object to appear. On the Insert menu, click New Object. Click the Create From File option button, and then select the file from the Browse dialog box. Click Insert, and then click OK. The contents of the file you selected are embedded into your document. To update the embedded object, double-click it, and then make the changes.
>
> For more information about embedding or other ways to share information between programs, refer to Windows 95 online Help. Or, refer to the *Step by Step* book on integrating Microsoft Office programs for details about sharing information among Microsoft Word, Microsoft Excel, Microsoft PowerPoint, and Microsoft Access.

Working with MS-DOS–Based Programs

In Windows 3.1, if you wanted to use MS-DOS commands or run an MS-DOS–based program, either you might have shut down Windows 3.1 to get back into the MS-DOS environment, or you might have used the MS-DOS Prompt icon to open an MS-DOS command window while Windows was still running.

Windows 95 has taken the place of MS-DOS as the operating system for your computer. Because of this, MS-DOS doesn't actually exist on your computer anymore. However, Windows 95 can completely simulate an MS-DOS environment for you. This way, you can run most MS-DOS–based programs.

You can do this by using the MS-DOS Prompt command on the Programs menu. This opens an MS-DOS command window in which you can run your MS-DOS–based programs. As in Windows 3.1, you can run the MS-DOS Prompt command in either a full screen or in a window on your Desktop. New in Windows 95 is an MS-DOS toolbar you can use to control the MS-DOS window and operations.

Open and adjust the MS-DOS window

In this exercise, you'll open and change the layout and size of an MS-DOS window.

1 Click Start. On the Start menu, point to Programs.

2 On the Programs menu, click MS-DOS Prompt.

An MS-DOS window opens on your Desktop. MS-DOS Prompt appears as a button on the taskbar. Your screen should look similar to the following illustration.

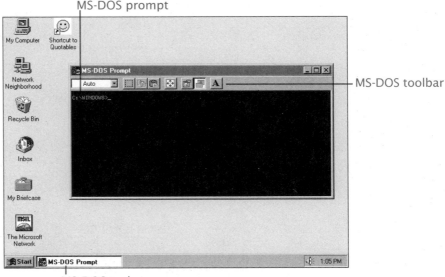

MS-DOS prompt

MS-DOS toolbar

MS-DOS task

Full Screen

3 Drag the MS-DOS Prompt title bar to move the window to a different location.

4 Click the Full Screen button to switch to full-screen mode.

The MS-DOS window fills the entire screen.

5 Press ALT+ENTER to restore both the Windows 95 Desktop and the MS-DOS window to their previous sizes and positions.

6 On the left side of the MS-DOS toolbar, open the Font list box.

When you click one of the sizes listed in the Font list box, the proper font proportions are displayed for the MS-DOS window size you choose.

7 Click 6x8.

The MS-DOS window changes in size to 6x8, and the font scales accordingly.

8 In the Font list box, click 7x12.

Use an MS-DOS–based text editing program

In this exercise, you'll start and use a built-in MS-DOS–based text editing program.

1 Be sure that the MS-DOS window is active.

2 At the MS-DOS prompt (C:\), type **dir** and then press ENTER.

The files on your hard disk and current folder appear in a list.

3 In the MS-DOS window, type **cd** and then press ENTER.

The CD command means "change directory." Adding the backslash (\) makes your folder the top folder on your hard disk.

You can use Edit and most other MS-DOS–based programs as you did when MS-DOS was the operating system. The difference is that now the program is running within a Windows 95 window.

4 Type **edit** and then press ENTER.

This starts an MS-DOS–based text editing program named "Edit." Your screen should look similar to the following illustration. Remember, you can switch to the full-screen mode by pressing ALT+ENTER or by clicking the Full Screen button on the MS-DOS toolbar.

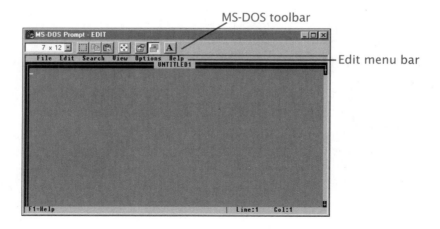

5 In the MS-DOS window running the Edit program, type the following letter. Press ENTER where indicated, because Edit does not provide the automatic wordwrap feature.

Dear Potential Investor: (ENTER)

(ENTER)

Thank you for your interest in Childs Play, Inc. stock. (ENTER)
In response to your request, I am enclosing last year's (ENTER)
annual plan and our prospectus.

6 In the menu bar, which is just below the MS-DOS toolbar, click File.

7 On the File menu, click Save.

The Save As dialog box appears, as shown in the following illustration.

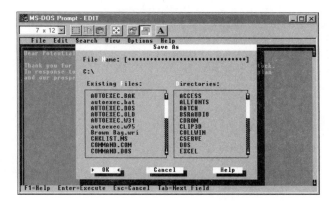

8 In the Directories box, double-click Windows 95 Practice. Use the scroll bar if necessary.

The Existing Files box changes to list the files currently in your Windows 95 Practice folder.

9 Click the File Name text area at the top of the dialog box, type **Investor Letter** and then click OK.

The letter is saved in the Windows 95 Practice folder.

Start a second MS-DOS–based program

In this exercise, you'll start a second MS-DOS–based program, in addition to the Edit program that is still running in its own MS-DOS window.

1 Click Start. On the Start menu, point to Programs.

2 On the Programs menu, click MS-DOS Prompt.

A second MS-DOS window opens on your Desktop, as shown in the following illustration.

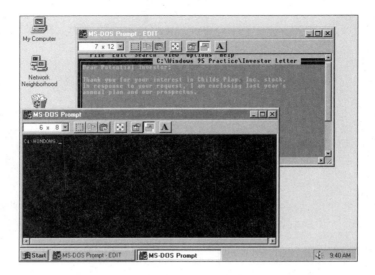

3   At the MS-DOS prompt, type **cd\window~1** and then press ENTER.

This changes your location to the Windows 95 Practice folder.

4   Type **dir** and then press ENTER.

A list of files and folders stored in this folder appear.

5   Type **db** and then press ENTER.

A display of a database appears. You are now running two MS-DOS–based programs at the same time.

Quit the MS-DOS–based programs and exit MS-DOS Prompt

In this exercise, you stop running the MS-DOS–based programs, return to the MS-DOS prompt, and exit the MS-DOS window.

1   In the new MS-DOS window running the DB program, press ESC.

The DB programs quits, and the MS-DOS prompt appears again. At this point, you can give other MS-DOS commands, run other MS-DOS–based programs, or exit the MS-DOS window.

2   At the MS-DOS prompt, type **exit** and then press ENTER.

One MS-DOS window closes. If you are running MS-DOS Prompt in full-screen mode, the screen changes back to the Windows 95 Desktop.

3   Click the remaining MS-DOS window running the Edit program to make it active.

4   On the File menu, click Exit.

The Investor Letter is saved, and the Edit program shuts down, displaying the MS-DOS prompt again.

5   At the MS-DOS prompt, type **exit** and then press ENTER to close the window.

Finish the lesson

1 Close all open windows by clicking the Close button in the upper-right corner of each window.

2 If any window is minimized, use the right mouse button to click the window's taskbar button, and then click Close.

3 Delete the Shortcut To Quotables from the Desktop by clicking the icon and pressing DELETE, or by dragging it to Recycle Bin.

   You are now ready to start the next lesson, or you can work on your own.

4 If you are finished using Windows 95 for now, on the Start menu click Shut Down, and then click Yes.

Lesson Summary

To	Do this
Find a program	Browse through My Computer, Explorer, or Find File.
Open a program	Double-click the program filename or icon.
Switch among open programs	Click the program name on the taskbar. *or* Hold down ALT and press TAB. While holding down ALT, continue to press TAB until you cycle to the program you want to open. Then release both keys. *or* Hold down ALT and press ESC to cycle through items on the taskbar.
Tile open windows on the Desktop	Use the right mouse button to click an empty space on the taskbar. On the shortcut menu, click Tile Vertically or Tile Horizontally.
Cascade open windows on the Desktop	Use the right mouse button to click an empty space on the taskbar. On the shortcut menu, click Cascade.
Copy and paste information between different programs	Use the Copy command to copy the information in the first program. Switch to the second program. Use the Paste command to paste the information in the location you want.

To	Do this
Open an MS-DOS window	Click Start. On the Start menu, click Programs, and then click MS-DOS Prompt.
Switch between a full-screen and an MS-DOS window	Press ALT+ENTER.
Change the size of an MS-DOS window	On the MS-DOS toolbar, click a size from the list box.
Enter an MS-DOS command in an MS-DOS window	Type the command at the MS-DOS prompt, and press ENTER.
Run an MS-DOS–based program	Type its start command at the MS-DOS prompt, and press ENTER.
Close the MS-DOS window	Type **exit**, and press ENTER.

For online information about	From the Help dialog box, click Index and then type
Locating program files	**programs, finding**
Switching between different open programs	**switching, between running programs**
Copying and pasting information between different programs	**copying, information from another document**
Giving MS-DOS commands and running MS-DOS–based programs	**MS-DOS programs**

For more information on	In *Introducing Microsoft Windows 95,* see
Locate program files	Chapter 1, "The Basics"

Preview of the Next Lessons

In Part 3, "Organizing and Communicating Your Work," you'll use Windows 95 to set up and maintain your files, folders, and disks. You'll learn how to communicate with other people through their computers. In Lesson 5, "Storing and Finding Files," you'll learn how to copy, move, rename, and delete your files and folders. You'll learn to format disks, and you'll practice different methods for locating your files.

Review & Practice

In the lessons in Part 2, "Doing Your Work with Windows 95," you used programs provided with Windows 95 as well as programs that you set up separately. If you want to practice these skills and test your understanding before you proceed with the lessons in Part 3, you can work through the Review & Practice section following this lesson.

Review & Practice

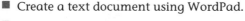

You will review and practice how to:

- Create a text document using WordPad.
- Create a drawing using Paint.
- Share information between different programs.
- Open an MS-DOS command window and run an MS-DOS–based program.

**Estimated time
30 min.**

You can practice the skills you learned in Part 2 by working through the steps in this Review & Practice section. You'll use the Microsoft Windows 95 accessories WordPad and Paint. You'll switch between open windows and copy information from one program to another.

Scenario

You are coordinating a series of "brown bag" lunch presentations for Childs Play employees. To publicize the events, you want to create a flyer, which will include an eye-catching drawing.

Step 1: Create a Text Document Using WordPad

First, you'll write and format the text for the brown bag lunch presentation flyer.

Create a new document

1 Use the Start button to start WordPad.

2   In the WordPad window, type the following text. Proof and correct the text as needed.

Announcing!
Brown Bag Lunch Presentations
every Wednesday, 12:00 noon until 12:50 PM
in the Recreation Center Assembly Room

Topics for April:
So You're Interested in Skin Diving and Scuba Diving?
Choosing a Child Care Center
Vacation Tips
Avoiding Strain at Work

For more information, call Leora at x1114

3   Save the document in your Windows 95 Practice folder, and name it **Brown Bag.wri**

Edit the document

1   Change the presentation topic "Vacation Tips" to **Vacation Planning Tips**
2   In the presentation topic "So You're Interested in Skin Diving and Scuba Diving?" delete the words "Skin Diving and".
3   Change the presentation topic "Avoiding Strain at Work" to **Avoiding Strain at Your Computer**
4   Save the changes.

Format the document

1   Select all the text in the document.
2   Center all the text. (Hint: Use the Center button on the format bar.)
3   Change the font of all the text in the document to Arial.
4   Change "Announcing" to 18-point bold type.
5   Change "Topics for April" to 14-point bold type.
6   Change the line that begins "For more information..." to italic.
7   Save your changes to the document.

For more information on	See
Using WordPad	Lesson 3

Step 2: *Create a Drawing Using Paint*

In this step, you will design the drawing to represent and help publicize the brown-bag lunch presentations.

Create a new graphic

1 Use the Start button to start Paint.

2 In the Paint window, use the Rectangle, Ellipse, and Line tools to create the following shapes.

3 Use the Text tool to type **Brown Bag Lunch Presentations** in the graphic. Change the font to 10-point bold italic type.

4 Use the Airbrush tool to create a brush effect, as shown in the following illustration.

5 Save the document in the Windows 95 Practice folder, and name it **Brown Bag Logo**

Select, copy, and paste shapes

1 Use the Select tool to select and copy the line design.

2 Paste the line design.

3 Move the pasted line design beneath the rectangle of the graphic, as shown in the following illustration.

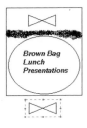

4 Save your changes.

Add color to the drawing

1 Use the Fill With Color tool to fill the areas of the drawing with the colors indicated in the following illustration.

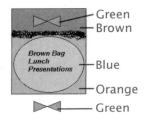

2 Save your changes.

For more information on	See
Using Paint	Lesson 3

Step 3: Share Information Between Programs

In this step, you'll copy the Paint drawing to the WordPad flyer.

1 Select and copy the entire Paint drawing.

2 Switch to the WordPad document.

3 Paste the drawing at the very top of the document.

4 Save the document.

5 Print the document.

For more information on	See
Sharing information between different programs	Lesson 4

Step 4:   Use an MS-DOS–Based Program

In this step, you'll open and adjust an MS-DOS command window and start the Edit program.

1   Open an MS-DOS command window.

2   Specify a 7x14 window and font size.

3   Start the MS-DOS text editor named Edit. (Hint: Type **edit** at the MS-DOS prompt.)

4   Type the following text, pressing ENTER wherever necessary to move to the next line.

Dear Brown Bag Lunch Presenters,

Attached is our schedule for the Brown Bag Lunch Presentations. Please call me if you need any special equipment for your presentation. Thank you!

Warm regards,

Leora Garcia

5   Save the file as **Presenter Letter** in your Windows 95 Practice folder.

6   Exit from the Edit program.

7   Exit from the MS-DOS command window.

For more information on	See
Using MS-DOS–based programs	Lesson 4

Finish the Review & Practice

1   Close all open windows.

2   If any window is minimized, use the right mouse button to click the window's taskbar button, and then click Close.

3   If you are finished using Windows 95 for now, on the Start menu click Shut Down, and then click Yes.

Organizing & Communicating Your Work

Storing and Finding Files

In this lesson you will learn how to:

Estimated time
45 min.

- Organize your files on your disks and in folders.
- Format new floppy disks to prepare them for use in your computer.
- Manage your files and folders by moving, copying, renaming, and deleting them.
- Find files that are stored throughout your computer system.

After you work at a job for a while, paperwork often starts to accumulate into one or more piles on your desk and around your office. This might be okay—until you can't find items you need right away. Your solution might be to organize your paperwork into different categories and then place the appropriate papers into labeled file folders. You might then place the folders into a filing cabinet. As you continued to work and accumulate more papers, you would put these papers exactly where they belong.

In the same way, after you work at your computer for a while, your files can accumulate in various places on your computer. In Microsoft Windows 3.1, you used File Manager to organize and manage your files. With Microsoft Windows 95, you can use My Computer or Windows Explorer to carry out these file management tasks.

In this lesson, you'll learn how to set up and maintain a computer filing system that suits the way you like to organize your files.

NOTE If you prefer, you can run the Windows 3.1 File Manager and Program Manager in the new Windows 95 environment. For File Manager, find and run the Winfile program file. For Program Manager, find and run the Progman program file. Both of these files are stored in your Windows folder, assuming you had installed Windows 95 over your previous version of Windows.

Setting Up Your Filing System

Whenever you create a new document in a program such as Paint or Microsoft Word, you can store the document on your computer's hard disk or on a floppy disk. As demonstrated in Lesson 3, "Using Windows 95 Accessories," you are no longer restricted to an eight-character maximum filename with a three-character maximum extension. In Windows 95, you can now make your filenames as long as you want them to be (up to 255 characters). You can also use spaces in your filenames.

Viewing Your Filing System

You can think of your hard disk as a huge filing cabinet built into your computer system. Likewise, your floppy disks are like small filing cabinets. Within either of these sizes of filing cabinets, you can store files and folders that, in turn, hold any number of individual files. Whenever you save a file you have created in a program, you can choose the disk and folder in which the file is to be stored. You can also move the file from one folder to another.

In Windows 3.1, you used directories to hold files. In Windows 95, directories are called folders. Whenever you set up a new program on your computer, the setup process creates a new folder on your hard disk. Then, all the program files that make the new program run are copied into that folder. The program files for one program are separate from the program files for another program. Because of this, even if you have a new computer, you probably already have a folder structure for your programs.

Just as you can have several manila file folders within a hanging file folder, you can have folders within folders on your computer system. With multiple levels of subfolders, you can organize your files very precisely and efficiently.

You can use My Computer or Windows Explorer to browse through your filing system. You can also change how you view the information in the windows.

Browse through your filing system with My Computer

In this exercise, you'll use My Computer to see which folders, files, and other resources you have on your computer. You'll also see how they're organized.

1 If your computer isn't already on, turn it on now. If you see the Welcome dialog box, read the tip and then click the Close button.

My Computer

Disk drive

Network drive

Folder

2 Double-click the My Computer icon.

The My Computer window appears. All disk drives on your computer are represented by a disk drive icon and name. If there are any established connections to other computers on the network, those computers are represented by a network drive icon and name.

3 Double-click the hard disk (C:) icon.

A new window appears, showing all top level folders and files stored on the hard disk.

4 Double-click the Windows 95 Practice folder.

A new window appears, showing all folders and files stored in the Windows 95 Practice folder. Folders, which hold other files, are represented by folder icons and names. Files are represented by the filename and an icon of the program in which the file was created.

If the icons in your window look different from these, click Large Icons on the View menu of the Windows 95 Practice window. Then, on the View menu, point to Arrange Icons and click Auto Arrange if it is not selected.

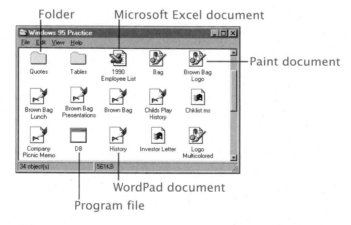

5 Double-click the Internal folder.

A new window appears, showing all files stored in the Internal folder. As you continue to open folders within folders, new windows open, listing each new folder's contents.

This action will only close a series of subfolder windows.

6 Close all open windows by holding down SHIFT while clicking the Close button of the active window.

Browse through your filing system with Windows Explorer

You can also browse through your filing system with the Windows 95 upgrade of File Manager called *Windows Explorer*. Just as in File Manager, Windows Explorer displays a double window, with different but corresponding information in the left and right windows. Windows Explorer provides a different view of the same information presented in the My Computer windows. In this exercise, you'll browse through your computer system files with Windows Explorer.

1 Click Start. On the Start menu, point to Programs, and then click Windows Explorer.

The Exploring window appears. The left window displays your computer's entire file structure, including any disk drives, folders, and established network connections in your computer system. The right window displays the names of the files and folders stored in the item selected in the left window.

Files in selected folder

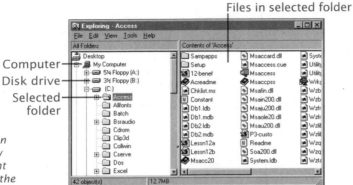

Computer—
Disk drive—
Selected—
folder

If the icons in your window look different from these, the view probably has a different setting. To match the settings in this lesson, click List on the View menu of the Exploring window.

2 In the left window, click the hard disk (C:).

The right window displays the names of the files, as well as any folders, stored there.

3 In the left window, double-click the Windows 95 Practice folder. If necessary, use the scroll bar.

The left window displays all folders stored in the Windows 95 Practice folder. The right window displays these folders as well as the names of the files stored in the Windows 95 Practice folder. These are the same folders and files you saw listed in My Computer.

4 In the left window, click the Marketing folder.

The right window displays all files stored in the Marketing folder.

5 Minimize the Windows Explorer window.

 TIP Most of your files do not show any filename extension. If you want all the extensions to show, on the View menu of either My Computer or Windows Explorer, click Options. In the Options dialog box, click the View tab. Click Hide MS-DOS File Extensions For The File Types That Are Registered to clear it. Click OK. All files will show their filename extensions.

Change the view of the My Computer windows

You can set up each of the My Computer windows to show only the information you want to see. In this exercise, you'll change the display of folders and files in the My Computer windows.

1   Double-click the My Computer icon.

2   Double-click the hard disk (C:) icon.

3   Click the View menu of the hard disk (C:) window. If Toolbar is not selected, click Toolbar; otherwise, press ESC to close the menu.

The toolbar appears in the hard disk (C:) window. This toolbar provides shortcuts for performing certain tasks and for changing window views. You can set each My Computer window to show or hide the toolbar. This setting remains in effect even after you close the window.

Maximize

4   Click the Maximize button on the hard disk (C:) window, and then click the List button on the toolbar.

Your toolbar should look similar to the following.

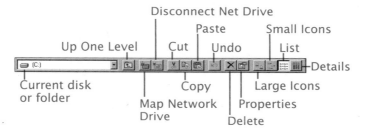

Large Icons

You can also click Large Icons on the View menu.

5   On the toolbar, click the Large Icons button.

The view changes from small icons to large icons.

6   On the toolbar, click the Small Icons button.

The view changes from large icons to small icons. This way, you can see more information in one window.

Small Icons

You can also click Small Icons on the View menu.

7   On the toolbar, click the Details button.

Details about each file or folder are listed in columns across the window. The details include the type of file and when the file was last modified.

Details

You can also click Details on the View menu.

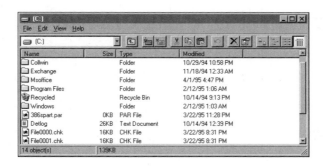

TIP In Windows Explorer, you can display the same toolbar and change the view. On the Windows Explorer toolbar or View menu, click Large Icons, Small Icons, List, or Details.

Organizing Your Files Within Folders

Depending on the nature of your work and the way you like to organize it, your filing scheme can take different forms. You might have a separate folder for each type of project, for example, letters, status reports, and budget forecasts. If you work with different clients, you might prefer to designate a separate folder for each client. If several individuals use one computer, as in a family or small business setting, you might want to set up a separate folder for each user. You can move files into the folders you create. You can also move or create folders within other folders. By adopting and adhering to a particular organizational scheme, you can keep your files in logical order for easy access.

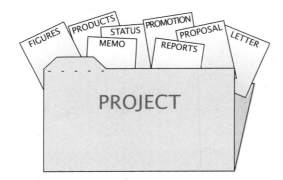

If you're having trouble finding your files in a folder...

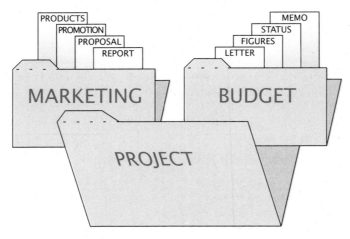

...you can organize your files into additional subfolders within the original folder.

Create folders for your new filing system

Suppose that after browsing through your computer filing system, you think of a more efficient way to organize your files: by grouping related files by tables, employee information, and product line information. In this exercise, you'll create these three folders for your new file organization scheme.

1 With the hard disk (C:) window still open, double-click the Windows 95 Practice folder icon.

The Windows 95 Practice folder window opens.

2 On the File menu of the Windows 95 Practice window, point to New, and then click Folder.

A new folder, named New Folder, appears at the bottom of the window. The name is selected so that you can replace it with the name you want.

3 Type **Tables** and then press ENTER.

The name of the folder changes to Tables.

4 Click an empty space in the Windows 95 Practice window.

This removes the selection from the Tables folder icon and allows you to create another folder. You cannot create a new folder when any item in the window is selected.

5 On the File menu, point to New, and then click Folder.

Another new folder appears in the window.

6 Type **Employee Information** and then press ENTER.

7 Following the same steps, create a new folder named **Product Line** within the Windows 95 Practice folder.

8 On the View menu, point to Arrange Icons, and then click By Name.

This rearranges all of your new icons so that the folders appear in alphabetical order at the top of the window.

 TIP You can also create new folders with Windows Explorer. In the left window, click the disk or folder in which you want the new folder to be stored. On the File menu, point to New, and then click Folder. A new folder appears at the bottom of the right window, and it is selected so that you can name it.

Move files into your new folders

Now suppose that you want to move files into the folders you just created. In this exercise, you'll move files from the Windows 95 Practice folder into the appropriate folders, using menu commands as well as the mouse.

107

1 With the Windows 95 Practice folder still open, click the Personnel Letter file icon once to select it. Use your scroll bar if necessary. All files are listed in alphabetical order.

You can also press CTRL+X to cut the selected file.

2 On the Edit menu, click Cut.

The Personnel Letter icon is dimmed, indicating that it's in the middle of a move operation.

3 Double-click the new Employee Information folder to open it. Use your scroll bar if necessary.

The Employee Information window appears.

You can also press CTRL+V to paste the selected file.

4 On the Edit menu of the Employee Information window, click Paste.

The Personnel Letter file appears in the Employee Information folder and then disappears from the Windows 95 Practice folder.

5 On the taskbar, click Windows 95 Practice.

The Windows 95 Practice folder appears.

6 In the Windows 95 Practice window, drag the 1995 Product Line icon to the Tables folder.

1995 Product Line moves to the Tables folder and is no longer listed in the Windows 95 Practice folder.

7 Double-click the Tables folder icon.

The Tables window appears, along with the moved file.

You can use these same procedures to move a folder inside another folder.

8 Move the following files into the indicated folders. Use the Cut and Paste commands on the Edit menu, or drag with the mouse.

Move this file	To this folder
Investment Portfolio	Employee Information
Employee Table	Tables
Product IDs	Tables
Employee Handbook	Employee Information
1996 Product Line	Product Line
Product Descriptions	Product Line

9 Close all open windows.

 TIP You can also move files with Windows Explorer. In the right window, click the file you want to move, and then on the Edit menu, click Cut. Double-click the folder to which you want to move the file, and then on the Edit menu, click Paste. Or, you can simply drag the file to the folder. You can move folders in the same way.

Managing Your Files and Folders

Even after you have all your files and folders where you want them, there might still be other changes you'd like to make to your files and folders. To make your filenames more descriptive, you can rename your files, or you can convert them from Windows 3.1 eight-character filenames to long filenames. You can also copy files to other folders or to the Desktop.

Another aspect of organizing and managing your files and folders is cleanup. You can delete old files you don't use anymore, and you can delete backup files or temporary files to free up space on your hard disk. The processes for renaming, copying, and deleting files in Windows 95 are similar to those used in Windows 3.1.

Rename files and folders

Suppose you want to rename several files to make the filenames more consistent with a new file naming scheme you've developed. In this exercise, you'll rename the Company Background file to "Childs Play History." You'll also rename the Bag file to "Brown Bag Lunch."

1 Double-click the My Computer icon, and then double-click the hard disk (C:) icon.

2 Double-click the Windows 95 Practice folder. If the icons appear jumbled from the previous exercise, point to Arrange Icons on the View menu, and then click By Name.

3 Click the Company Background file once to select it.

4 On the File menu, click Rename.

On the Company Background file icon, the filename is highlighted and the insertion point appears at the end of the filename.

5 Type **Childs Play History** to change the filename, and then press ENTER.

6 Use the right mouse button to click the Bag WordPad file.

The file is selected and a pop-up menu appears.

7 On the pop-up menu, click Rename.

The filename is highlighted, and the insertion point appears at the end of the filename.

You can use these same procedures to rename a folder.

8 Type **Brown Bag Lunch** and then press ENTER.

The filename changes.

TIP You can also rename files with Windows Explorer. In the right window, click the file you want to rename, and then from the File menu, click Rename. Or, use the right mouse button to click the file, and then click Rename.

Copy files to another folder

Suppose you have files in one folder and you want to put exact copies of these files in another folder. In this exercise, you'll copy files between folders.

1   With the Windows 95 Practice folder still open, click the Sports Products List file icon once to select it.

You can also press CTRL+C to copy and then CTRL+V to paste the selected file. Or, use the right mouse button to click the window, and then click Copy or Paste on the pop-up menu.

2   On the Edit menu, click Copy.

The Sports Products List file is copied to the computer's memory, but nothing changes on the screen.

3   Double-click the Product Line folder.

4   On the Edit menu of the Product Line window, click Paste.

A copy of the Sports Products List file appears in the Product Line folder.

5   If the icons appear jumbled, point to Arrange Icons on the View menu, and then click By Name. If you always want your icons to be neatly arranged in a window, point to Arrange Icons on the window's View menu, and then click Auto Arrange.

6   On the taskbar, click Windows 95 Practice and then click an empty area in the Windows 95 Practice window to deselect the folder icon.

7   In the Windows 95 Practice folder, hold down CTRL and drag Chklist.ms to the Letters folder until the folder icon changes color.

While you're dragging, your mouse pointer displays a plus sign. The plus sign appears when you hold down CTRL, indicating that you are copying rather than moving the file.

You can use these same procedures to copy a folder into another folder.

8   Double-click the Letters folder.

The Letters folder opens, and it now includes the Chklist.ms file.

 TIP   You can also copy files with Windows Explorer. In the right window, click the file you want to copy, and then from the Edit menu, click Copy. In the left or right window, click the folder where you want to place the copied file, and then from the Edit menu, click Paste. Or, you can hold down CTRL and drag the file to the folder.

Delete files

Suppose you have some files that are old backups and you don't need them taking up space on your hard disk anymore. In this exercise, you'll delete files using Recycle Bin.

1   On the taskbar, click Windows 95 Practice.

The Windows 95 Practice folder appears.

Recycle Bin

2 Drag the 1990 Employee List to the Recycle Bin icon on your Desktop. If necessary, position or minimize windows to move them out of the way.

The 1990 Employee List file no longer appears in the Windows 95 Practice folder. You have just moved it to Recycle Bin, a holding area for files and folders you no longer need.

3 In the Windows 95 Practice window, use the right mouse button to click the Retirement Planning Backup file.

A pop-up menu appears.

4 On the pop-up menu, click Delete.

The Confirm File Delete dialog box appears.

You can also delete a file by selecting it and pressing DELETE on your keyboard.

5 Click Yes.

The Retirement Planning Backup file disappears from the Windows 95 Practice folder and is placed in Recycle Bin.

6 From the Windows 95 Practice window, drag the Worksheet folder to the Recycle Bin icon.

The Worksheet folder is deleted. Deleted items stay in Recycle Bin until you explicitly empty it. You might prefer to keep deleted items as insurance against accidental deletions or other mishaps.

TIP You can also use Recycle Bin to delete files and folders from Windows Explorer.

Recover deleted files from Recycle Bin

Suppose you changed your mind about a file or folder you deleted. If you have not yet emptied Recycle Bin, you can retrieve and re-use any item stored there. In this exercise, you'll recover deleted files from Recycle Bin.

1 Double-click the Recycle Bin icon.

The Recycle Bin window appears, listing all files, folders, and other items deleted since the last time Recycle Bin was emptied.

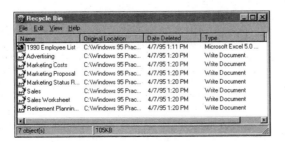

To recover the last item deleted, you can also click the Undo Delete command on the Edit menu of the Recycle Bin window.

2   From the Recycle Bin window, drag 1990 Employee List back to the Windows 95 Practice folder.

The 1990 Employee List file appears in the folder again, and you can use the file as if it had never been deleted.

3   Close the Recycle Bin window.

TIP   Another way to recover files from Recycle Bin is to click the item, and then on the Recycle Bin File menu, click Restore. The file returns to whatever folder it was deleted from, even if the folder is not currently open.

Empty Recycle Bin

Items in Recycle Bin take up space on your hard disk. If you're deleting files and folders to make more room on your hard disk, you need to empty Recycle Bin. In this exercise, you'll delete selected files in Recycle Bin from the hard disk. You'll also empty all the items in Recycle Bin.

1   Double-click the Recycle Bin icon.

The Recycle Bin window opens, displaying a list of all items deleted since the last time Recycle Bin was emptied. The status bar at the bottom of the Recycle Bin window indicates the number of objects in Recycle Bin and how much disk space these objects occupy.

2   Hold down CTRL and click any three nonadjacent items in the list.

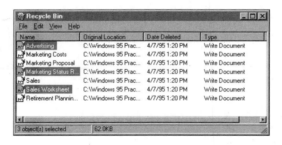

You can also select multiple adjacent items by holding down SHIFT, clicking the first item, and then clicking the last item in the series. All items between the first and last item are selected.

By holding down CTRL, you can select several nonadjacent items at one time in any list.

3   On the File menu of Recycle Bin, click Delete.

The Confirm Multiple File Delete dialog box appears.

4   Click Yes.

The three items are completely deleted from Recycle Bin and from your hard disk.

5   On the File menu, click Empty Recycle Bin.

The Confirm Multiple File Delete dialog box appears.

6 Click Yes.

All the contents of Recycle Bin are removed from your hard disk.

7 Close all open windows.

 TIP You can also empty Recycle Bin without opening it. Use the right mouse button to click Recycle Bin. On the pop-up menu, click Empty Recycle Bin.

Managing Your Disks

Although your hard disk is probably the primary storage device you use every day, you might use floppy disks as well. It's wise to copy your document files onto a floppy disk periodically so that you have backup files in case your hard disk malfunctions. In addition, you might have document files stored on floppy disks that you want to transfer onto your hard disk. You can use Windows Explorer or My Computer to manage the information on your disks in these ways. You can also format a new floppy disk to prepare it for initial use.

Backing Up Files onto a Floppy Disk

You can use floppy disks to make backup copies of the files stored on your hard disk. If you copy your files onto a new, blank floppy disk, you must first be sure that it is formatted. Then you can copy the files from your hard disk onto the floppy disk.

Format a new floppy disk

Suppose you have just bought a new box of unformatted floppy disks. In this exercise, you'll format a new floppy disk, to prepare it for use in your computer. A disk needs to be formatted only once.

 WARNING The formatting process erases any information previously stored on the floppy disk.

---

1 Place a new floppy disk (or a used one containing information you no longer want) in the appropriate floppy disk drive (3.5-inch or 5.25-inch). Be sure you know whether it is a double-density or a high-density floppy disk.

2 Double-click the My Computer icon.

The My Computer window appears.

You can also use the right mouse button to click the disk drive icon, and then on the pop-up menu, click Format.

3 Click the icon for the disk drive that contains the floppy disk you want to format.

Be sure to click just once to select the icon, rather than open the disk.

4 On the File menu, click Format.

The Format dialog box appears.

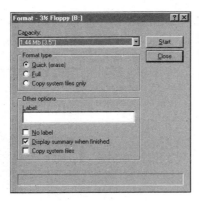

5 In the Capacity list box, specify the capacity of the floppy disk.

The capacity depends on whether the floppy disk is a double-density (DD) or high-density (HD) disk.

6 Under Format Type, click Full.

The Quick (Erase) option erases all information from a formatted floppy disk. The Copy System Files Only option copies system files to a formatted floppy disk that's already formatted. You can start up your system with a disk that contains system files.

If you want to format a disk and then copy system files onto it, click Copy System Files under Other Options.

7 Under Other Options, be sure that the Label text box is blank and that Display Summary When Finished is checked, and then click Start.

In the Formatting bar at the bottom of the Format dialog box, tick marks indicate the status of the formatting process, which might take a couple minutes. When the bar is filled in, the formatting is complete, and the Format Results dialog box appears.

8 In the Format Results dialog box, click Close.

The Format dialog box appears again. If you wanted to format several floppy disks of the same size and capacity, you could now insert another floppy disk and click Start again. This is useful when you're formatting an entire box of new floppy disks.

9 In the Format dialog box, click Close. Remove the floppy disk from the disk drive, and label it "Windows 95 Disk and Briefcase Practice." Then, reinsert the disk for use in the next exercise.

 TIP You can also format floppy disks with Windows Explorer. In Windows Explorer, use the right mouse button to click the name of the floppy disk drive in the left window. From the pop-up menu, click Format.

Copy files and folders from the hard disk to a floppy disk

Now that your floppy disk is formatted, you're ready to copy files onto it from your hard disk. You do this when you want to make a backup of your files in case of a malfunction or to transfer files to another computer. In this exercise, you'll copy files stored in your Windows 95 Practice folder on your hard disk and store them on your floppy disk.

To duplicate floppy disks, select the icon in the My Computer window for the floppy disk you want to copy, and then click Copy Disk from the File menu.

TIP You can also make periodic backups of all the files on your hard disk by using the Backup system accessory. From the Accessories menu, point to System Tools, and then click Backup. Click OK in the Welcome window to display the Microsoft Backup Wizard. Follow the steps through the Wizard. You can use Backup to back up files to floppy disks or to make duplicate floppy disks.

1 Open the hard disk (C:) and the Windows 95 Practice folder.

2 In the Windows 95 Practice folder, click Brown Bag Lunch.

3 On the File menu, point to Send To, and then click the disk drive name.

The Brown Bag Lunch file is copied to the floppy disk drive.

4 On the taskbar, click My Computer, and then double-click the floppy disk drive icon, either drive A (A:) or B (B:).

The floppy disk drive window appears and displays the icon for the Brown Bag Lunch file.

Using this same process, you can also copy files and folders from a floppy disk to the hard disk.

5 On the taskbar, click the Windows 95 Practice button.

6 Arrange the floppy drive window so that at least part of it is visible under the Windows 95 Practice window.

7 From the Windows 95 Practice window, drag the Brown Bag Presentations file to the floppy disk window.

When dragging between disks, the item is automatically copied. If you want to move an item, hold down SHIFT while you drag.

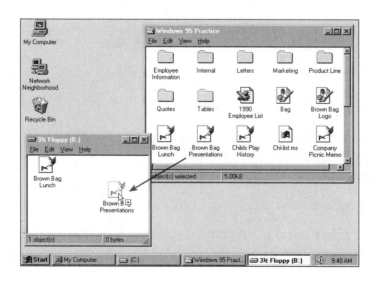

The plus sign in your mouse pointer indicates that you're copying the file to the floppy disk. When dragging between a floppy disk and the hard disk, the item is automatically copied rather than moved. Brown Bag Presentations is copied to the floppy disk window.

You can use these same procedures to move a folder into another folder.

8   Close all open windows.

 TIP   You can also copy files between the hard disk and floppy disk drive with Windows Explorer. In Windows Explorer, select the file to be copied. From the File menu, click Send To, and then click the floppy disk drive name. Or, drag the file to the drive icon.

Locating Your Files

Up to this point, you've been locating your files by browsing through My Computer or Windows Explorer. When you know the general vicinity of a file, that is, which folder a file might be in, browsing like this is probably the most convenient way to find the files you're looking for. But what do you do if you know part of the filename but don't have any idea where it might be on the hard disk?

In Windows 3.1 File Manager, you could search for files stored throughout your computer. You can do the same thing in Windows 95 to help you locate either *program files* or *document files*. Program files run programs such as WordPad, Paint, and Microsoft PowerPoint. Document files are the work, or data, you create when you use one of these programs. With Windows 95, you can also quickly browse through the contents of a file without opening it completely.

Find a document or program file

Suppose you have created a file, but you don't remember which folder you saved it in. Or, suppose you have set up a new program, but you didn't add a shortcut to it on the Programs menu or the Desktop, and now you don't know where the new program is. In this exercise, you'll find and open a document file using the Find command. You'll also find a program file and then start the program.

1   Click Start. On the Start menu, point to Find.

2   On the Find menu, click Files Or Folders.

The Find dialog box appears.

3   Be sure that the Name & Location tab is active.

4   In the Named box, type **wordpad** and then click Find Now.

All files throughout your hard disk that have "WordPad" as part of its filename are listed at the bottom of the dialog box. Also listed are the folders in which the files are stored, the file sizes in kilobytes (KB), and the file types.

5   Double-click the WordPad program file (application type) in the Find dialog box.

WordPad starts.

6   Minimize WordPad.

7   Click New Search in the Find window, and then click OK.

The Find fields are cleared.

The Named list box maintains a list of your previous search operations.

8   In the Named box, type **logo** and then click Find Now.

All files throughout your hard disk that have "logo" as part of their filenames are listed at the bottom of the dialog box.

9   In the list of files, scroll to Dept Logo Color and double-click it.

The Paint program starts, and then the Dept Logo Color file appears in its window.

TIP   You can also search by file type or file contents. In the Find dialog box, click the Advanced tab. In the Of Type list box, select the type of file you want to find. In the Containing Text box, type a key word or phrase. The system will search for all files of the type you selected that contain the key word or phrase you entered.

Quickly view a document file

If you're viewing a file list in the Find dialog box, a My Computer window, or Windows Explorer, you might like to briefly scan the contents of a few files. This can be more efficient than starting the programs and then opening the files. In this exercise, you'll use Quick View to browse through the contents of document files.

If the Quick View option is missing, see "Matching the Exercises" in the Appendix.

1   On the taskbar, click Find: Files Named Logo.

The Find dialog box appears.

2   In the list box at the bottom of the dialog box, click Windows Logo and then, from the File menu, click Quick View.

The file appears in a window. You can view a file, but not edit it, when it's displayed in a Quick View window.

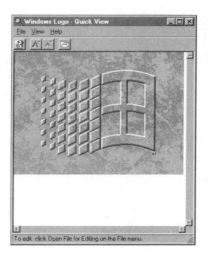

3 Close the Quick View window.

4 Use the right mouse button to click Logo Multicolored in the list of files.

A pop-up menu appears.

5 Click Quick View.

Logo Multicolored appears in a Quick View window.

6 On the File menu, click Open File For Editing.

Paint opens and now, if you wanted to, you could edit the logo.

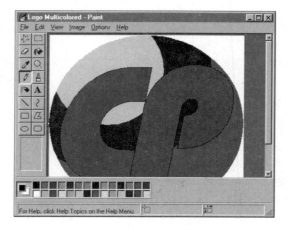

TIP The Quick View command is also available in any My Computer window and in Windows Explorer. Click the file you want to view, and then from the File menu, click Quick View. You can also use the pop-up menu.

Finish the lesson

In the following steps, you will return your computer to the settings it had when you started this lesson. You will also close any open windows.

Small Icons

1 Double-click the My Computer icon and then double-click the hard disk (C:). On the toolbar, click Small Icons.

2 Close all open windows by clicking the Close button in the upper-right corner of each window.

3 If any window is minimized, use the right mouse button to click the window's taskbar button, and then click Close.

You are now ready to start the next lesson, or you can work on your own.

4 If you are finished using Windows 95 for now, on the Start menu click Shut Down, and then click Yes.

Lesson Summary

To	Do this
Browse through your computer filing system with My Computer	Double-click the My Computer icon. Double-click any disk drives and folders in which you want to browse for files.
Browse through your computer filing system with Windows Explorer	Click Start, point to Programs, and then click Windows Explorer. In the left window, click the disk drive and any folders in which you want to browse. In the right window, view the files stored on the disk drive or folder selected in the left window.
Change the view of the Windows Explorer or My Computer window	On the Windows Explorer or My Computer window, click the View menu, and then make the choices you want to customize the window.
Create a new folder	Open the disk drive or folder in which you want the new folder to be stored. On the File menu, point to New, and then click Folder. Type a name for the new folder, and then press ENTER.

To	Do this
Move a file to another folder	Click the name of the file to be moved. On the Edit menu, click Cut. Open the folder in which you want to move the folder. On the Edit menu, click Paste. *or* Drag the file to the folder in which you want to move the file.
Rename a file or folder	Use the right mouse button to click the file you want to rename. On the pop-up menu, click Rename. Type the new name, and then press ENTER.
Copy a file to another folder	Hold down CTRL, and drag the file you want to copy to the new location.
Delete a file	Drag the file to the Recycle Bin icon on the Desktop. *or* Click the file, press DELETE, and then click Yes.
Recover a deleted file	Open Recycle Bin, and then drag the file you want to recover to the folder, disk drive, or Desktop. *or* Open Recycle Bin, click the file you want to recover, and then on the Recycle Bin File menu, click Restore.
Empty Recycle Bin	Open Recycle Bin, and then from the File menu, click Empty Recycle Bin.
Format a new floppy disk	Insert the floppy disk, and use My Computer or Windows Explorer to select the disk drive. On the File menu, click Format. Specify the capacity of the floppy disk, click Full, and then click Start.
Copy files and folders from the hard disk to a floppy disk	In My Computer or Windows Explorer, select the files or folders you want to copy. On the File menu, point to Send To, and then click the appropriate disk drive name.

To	Do this
Find a program file	Click Start, point to Find, and then click Files Or Folders. On the Name & Location tab, type the program name. Click the Advanced tab. In the Of Type list box, click Application, and then click Find Now.
Find a document file	Click Start, point to Find, and then click Files Or Folders. In the Name & Location tab, type all or part of the filename in the Name box, and then click Find Now.
View a document file with Quick View	In the Find dialog box, My Computer window, or Windows Explorer, use the right mouse button to click the document file you want to quickly view. On the pop-up menu, click Quick View.

For online information about	From the Help dialog box, click Index and then type
Browsing with My Computer or Windows Explorer	**browsing, through folders on your computer**
Creating and using folders	**folders**
Copying files and folders	**copying, files or folders**
Moving files and folders	**moving, files or folders**
Deleting files and folders	**deleting, files or folders**
Using Recycle Bin	**Recycle Bin**
Formatting floppy disks	**formatting, disks**
Finding files	**Find command, using**
Using Quick View	**Quick View**
Starting and using File Manager	**File Manager**

For more information on	In *Introducing Microsoft Windows 95*, see
Finding and viewing files	Chapter 1, "The Basics"
Browsing through files on your computer	Chapter 2, "Beyond the Basics"
Creating and using folders	Chapter 2, "Beyond the Basics"
Copying, moving, and deleting files and folders	Chapter 2, "Beyond the Basics"

Preview of the Next Lesson

In the next lesson, you will learn how to work with other computers, whether your computer is connected to other computers through a network system or you're accessing them via telecommunication. You'll synchronize files with My Briefcase, use information on a network computer, send and receive electronic mail, and log on to The Microsoft Network.

Communicating
with Computers

In this lesson you will learn how to:

Estimated time
50 min.

- Synchronize files that are duplicated on different computers with My Briefcase.
- Share files and folders with other users on your network.
- Create, send, and receive mail messages with Microsoft Exchange and the Inbox.
- Connect to other computers through telephone lines by using Dial-Up Networking or HyperTerminal.
- Sign up for The Microsoft Network online service.

Most people don't work in a vacuum. Business is often conducted in teams, or work-groups. Members of these teams might share information by face-to-face meetings or by the telephone. They might also exchange memos, reports, and other documents. There is often a common area, such as a library or a media resource center, where information for general use is available.

You can also use your computer to exchange information with your co-workers. In addition, you can look up resource information stored on other computers to help you accomplish tasks. With Microsoft Windows 95, you can share files among different computers and control the version changes on those computers.

In this lesson, you'll learn how to work with other computers at various locations. You'll work with computers connected together on a network. You'll also learn how to "call" another computer by telephone to access additional resources for your work.

There are several methods to communicate and exchange information with other computers. The following table summarizes these methods, the situations in which you would use them, and the additional hardware or software you need.

When you want to	Use this method	You need this type of additional hardware or software
Transfer and synchronize files on an alternate computer, such as a home computer or a laptop	Copy files to My Briefcase	None
Share your files with other users on your network	Designate your information as a shared resource	Network hardware and software
Access shared files available on other computers on your network	Map to a network drive, and then browse through and open the shared files	Network hardware and software
Call and access the files on another computer running Windows 95	Connect to the other computer with Dial-Up Networking	Windows 95, a modem on both computers, and remote network access software on the host PC.
Call and log on to an online service, a bulletin board, or a computer running a different operating system	Connect to the other computer with HyperTerminal	Modem
Find information on news, sports, weather, or technical issues, download software programs, or access the Internet	Connect to The Microsoft Network	Modem

The following sections explain these methods in greater detail.

Going Mobile with My Briefcase

You might not always work in one place. For example, you might work in different locations within a company, or traveling might be a part of your job. You might occasionally take work home or work at home a few days a week. When traveling between locations, you probably use a briefcase to carry your paper files. In the same way, you can copy electronic files and folders into *My Briefcase* and then move My Briefcase onto a floppy disk for transfer and use on another computer.

My Briefcase is similar to a folder in that My Briefcase can hold folders and files. You can copy the folders and files you want to use on another computer into My Briefcase, move My Briefcase onto a floppy disk, and then use the disk on the other computer. This is useful when you need to transfer files between two computers—for example, between a work computer and a home computer, or between a desktop system and a laptop system.

However, My Briefcase does more than just transfer files. And, it's more than just a type of folder. With My Briefcase, you can *synchronize* duplicate files that are stored in two locations. My Briefcase keeps track of the duplicate files and alerts you when one of the files is different from the other. My Briefcase also prompts you to update a file by replacing the older version of the file with the newer version. This prevents you from inadvertently working on an older version of a file that doesn't include the updates you made to the file on the other computer. By using My Briefcase, you can be more confident that your files are current and synchronized properly.

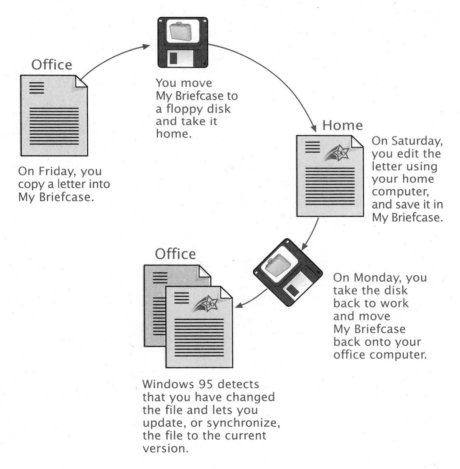

Office

On Friday, you copy a letter into My Briefcase.

You move My Briefcase to a floppy disk and take it home.

Home

On Saturday, you edit the letter using your home computer, and save it in My Briefcase.

On Monday, you take the disk back to work and move My Briefcase back onto your office computer.

Office

Windows 95 detects that you have changed the file and lets you update, or synchronize, the file to the current version.

In the following exercises, you will be using My Briefcase to create duplicate sets of files that are synchronized with one another.

NOTE If you do not see the My Briefcase icon on your Desktop, that means it is not currently set up on your computer. For information on how to set up My Briefcase on your computer, refer to "Changing Your Setup" in the Appendix.

Copy files into My Briefcase

Suppose you have a computer at home and one at your office. Sometimes you bring your office files home to work on a special project. In this exercise, you'll copy files on your "office" computer into My Briefcase for use on your "home" computer. (Your home computer can be any other computer running Windows 95, or, if another computer is not available, you can use your own computer.)

1   If your computer isn't already on, turn it on now. If you see the Welcome dialog box, read the tip and then click the Close button.

2   Using either My Computer or Windows Explorer, open the Windows 95 Practice folder on the hard disk.

My Briefcase

3   Use the right mouse button to drag the Product Table file to the My Briefcase icon.

A pop-up menu appears.

4   On the pop-up menu, click Make Sync Copy.

A synchronized copy of the Product Table file is created in My Briefcase.

5   On the Desktop, double-click the My Briefcase icon.

If you see the Welcome To The Windows Briefcase window, read it and then click Finish. The My Briefcase window appears, as shown in the following illustration.

If your screen looks different from this illustration, refer to "Matching the Exercises" in the Appendix.

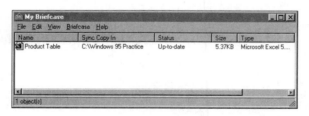

6   From the Windows 95 Practice folder, use the right mouse button to drag the Internal folder to the My Briefcase window, and then click Make Sync Copy.

Rearrange and scroll through windows as necessary. Synchronized copies of the Internal folder and its contents are created in My Briefcase.

7   Close the My Briefcase window.

Move My Briefcase to a floppy disk

In this exercise, you'll transfer My Briefcase to a floppy disk for transfer to your home computer.

NOTE In the following exercises, you will use the floppy disk that you formatted earlier in Lesson 5, "Storing and Finding Files." If you have not done Lesson 5, obtain a formatted floppy disk that you can use in one of your floppy disk drives, and label it "Windows 95 Disk and Briefcase Practice."

1 Insert the floppy disk labeled "Windows 95 Disk and Briefcase Practice" into the appropriate disk drive of your office computer.

2 On the taskbar, click the My Computer button or the Exploring button.

The My Computer window or Exploring window appears.

3 Use the right mouse button to drag the My Briefcase icon from the Desktop to your floppy disk drive icon in either My Computer or Windows Explorer.

A pop-up menu appears.

4 On the pop-up menu, click Move Here.

My Briefcase and all the files contained there are moved to the floppy disk. The My Briefcase icon disappears from your Desktop.

The contents of My Briefcase must fit entirely on the disk on which it is stored. My Briefcase does not span multiple disks.

5 Double-click the floppy disk drive icon.

The My Briefcase icon appears among the list of other items on your floppy disk.

6 Double-click My Briefcase to open it.

The file and folder you copied to My Briefcase appear.

7 Close all open windows.

8 Remove the floppy disk from the drive.

You could now take the files on the Briefcase disk and use them on your home computer running Windows 95.

Edit the files in My Briefcase

In this exercise, you'll edit one of the files in My Briefcase on your home computer.

 NOTE Try the following exercise on another Windows 95 computer, if one is available. Otherwise, you can use your own computer.

1. Insert the floppy disk labeled "Windows 95 Disk and Briefcase Practice" into the floppy disk drive of your home computer.

2. Using My Computer or Windows Explorer, open the drive in which your floppy disk is inserted.

3. Double-click the My Briefcase icon to open it.

4. Double-click the Internal folder to open it.

5. Double-click the 1996 Product Line file to open it in WordPad.

6. At the top of the document, add the following title text:

   Childs Play

   1996 Product Line

   Marketing Proposal

7. On the toolbar, click the Save button.

8. Close all open windows, including the 1996 Product Line document window.

9. Remove the floppy disk from the drive.

Save

 NOTE You can also move My Briefcase from the floppy disk to the hard disk of another computer, and then you can work on the files there. If there is already a My Briefcase icon on the other computer, you can move My Briefcase from the floppy disk into a folder on your hard disk drive. Or, you can add the contents of the new My Briefcase to the existing one. If there are identical files on the existing My Briefcase, you are alerted and given the option to replace the contents of the existing My Briefcase with the new contents. Either way, when you have finished editing the files, you would move My Briefcase back to the floppy disk.

Update the duplicate files with My Briefcase

In this exercise, you'll synchronize the files on your office computer with the files stored on My Briefcase.

1. Insert the floppy disk labeled "Windows 95 Disk and Briefcase Practice" into the floppy disk drive of your office computer.

2. Using either My Computer or Windows Explorer, open the floppy disk drive.

3. Use the right mouse button to drag the My Briefcase icon from the floppy disk drive to an empty area on your Desktop, and then on the pop-up menu, click Move Here.

   The files and folder in My Briefcase are moved from the floppy disk to the Desktop. The My Briefcase icon disappears from the floppy disk window.

4. Close all open windows.

5   Double-click the My Briefcase icon to open it.

The folder and file are listed, and the status of the Internal folder says "Needs Updating."

6   Double-click the Internal folder.

The Internal window appears and shows that the Product Line file needs updating.

7   On the Briefcase menu, click Update All.

The files in My Briefcase are compared with the corresponding files on your office computer. The Update My Briefcase window appears, indicating that the 1996 Product Line file in My Briefcase has been modified and should replace the un-modified version on the hard disk.

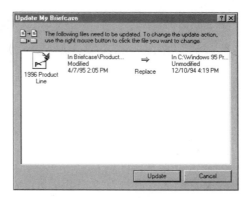

8   Click Update.

The newer version in My Briefcase replaces the older version on the hard disk. Now all the files in My Briefcase and on your office computer are synchronized. The Internal window in My Briefcase indicates that the files and folder are up to date.

9   Close any open windows.

Working with Computers on a Network

Many workplaces connect all their computers together on a *network* so that they can share information. A network is a system of multiple computers that use special networking programs to share resources among different connected computers. Networks are an efficient way of using hardware and software, because resources can be shared. For example, instead of each computer being connected to its own printer, five or ten comput-ers can share one printer on a network. Software and other files that everyone on the network uses can be stored on a central computer, called a *server* (or *file server*), that all users can access. Document folders containing files that need to be shared among work teams can be accessed through the network. Users on the network can send electronic mail, or *e-mail*, to each other to make communication more efficient.

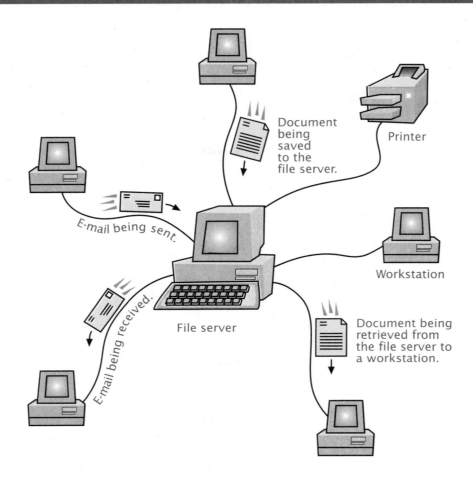

NOTE   The exercises in this section work only if your computer is part of a network. Your computer must include a network interface card and be physically cabled to other computers on the network. If you need to install and set up network and file sharing services, double-click the Network icon in Control Panel, and complete the Network dialog box. If your computer is not on a network, you can skip this section and go on to the section "Working with Computers Across Phone Lines."

Viewing the Resources in Your Network

Just as My Computer displays the folders and files you have stored on the computer sitting on your desk, Network Neighborhood displays the outside resources that are available in the wider computing community of your network. Such resources can include other computers, disk drives, folders, files, and printers. You can use Network Neighborhood to browse through, open, explore, and use the resources available throughout your network.

Network Neighborhood works in a similar manner as My Computer—the difference is that it displays the contents of multiple computers, rather than just the contents of a single computer.

You can establish connections with other computers on your network and then browse through the files on those computers that have *shared resources*—folders that users on the network have identified as being available to other users.

Browse through Network Neighborhood

Suppose you want to see what other computers and network resources are available beyond your current mapped drives. In this exercise, you'll use Network Neighborhood to view the other available network resources.

*Network
Neighborhood*

1 Double-click the Network Neighborhood icon.

The Network Neighborhood window appears, showing the computers on your network. The Entire Network icon also appears. Your screen might look similar to the following illustration.

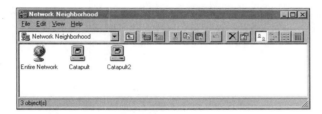

2 Double-click the Entire Network icon.

The Entire Network window appears. Your screen might look similar to the following illustration.

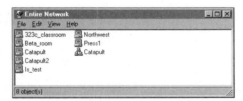

3 Continue to browse through the network.

If you find a computer to which you want to connect, double-click the computer's icon in Network Neighborhood, and then choose a shared folder from the window.

4 Close all open windows.

Using Information from Networked Computers

You can establish connections with other computers on your network and then browse through the files on those computers that have *shared resources*—folders that users on the network have identified as being available to a select group of other users.

To access folders on another computer, you must designate a shared folder or drive on that computer as a drive available to your computer. This process is called *mapping*. You can map a shared folder or drive by using either My Computer or Network Neighborhood. When you do this, you can simply double-click the network drive icon to view and use the files and folders stored there, just as if the network drive were a disk drive physically connected to your computer.

When you map a network drive, you need to indicate the drive letter you want to use. Drive A, and sometimes drive B, is used by your floppy disk drives. Drive C is used by your hard disk. You might have used other drive letters already if you have an additional hard disk, a CD-ROM drive, a backup tape drive, or if other network drive designations have already been established. The Map Network Drive dialog box lists all available drive letters.

When you map a network drive, you also need to indicate the *path*—the name and location of the computer and folder to which you're connecting. The path is entered in the following format: *computername**foldername*

For example, if the name of the computer is Accounts and the name of the folder you want to connect to is named Midwest, the path is \\accounts\midwest. You can find the names of shared computers, folders, and other shared resources by browsing through the Network Neighborhood.

You might find it efficient to map to all the network drives you use regularly. Then whenever you need to access a network drive, it's readily available. The network drive icons appear in either My Computer or Network Neighborhood—wherever you mapped the icon.

Map to a network drive

In this exercise, you'll map to a network drive so that you can connect to and use resources on other computers on the network.

1   Open My Computer.

2   Be sure that the toolbar appears in the My Computer window. If the toolbar is not showing, on the View menu, click Toolbar.

3   On the toolbar, click the Map Network Drive button to display the Map Network Drive dialog box.

*Map Network
Drive*

4   In the Drive list box, type **W** or select "W" from the list of available drives.

This indicates the drive designation you want for the computer and folder to which you're connecting. If the W drive is already being used by another device or network connection, choose a drive designation that is not being used.

5   In the Path list box, select a path to any computer and folder on your network, and then click OK.

The path indicates the network location of the computer and folder to which you want to connect. If there are no paths in the list box, find out from your network administrator the name of a computer and folder on the network to which you can connect.

6   If a password is required for you to connect to this computer and folder, the password dialog box appears. Type the password and then click OK.

The folder on the other computer connects, or maps, to your computer across the network. A new network drive icon appears in the My Computer window, as shown in the following illustration.

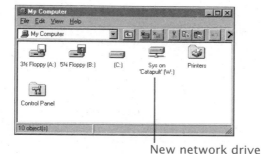

New network drive

As soon as you map to a shared folder, its window opens to display its contents.

 TIP   You don't have to map a network drive to connect to a network resource. You can also open any network resource with the Run command on the Start menu. In the Run dialog box, type the path in the *computername**foldername* format, and then click OK.

View information on another computer

Now that you have mapped your network drive, you can look at the files stored there. In this exercise, you'll browse through and view files that are stored on another computer in your network.

1   Be sure that Drive W, the network drive you connected in the previous exercise, is open. If it is not open, double-click its drive icon in the My Computer window.

2 Browse through the folders and files in Drive W, and open a file that was created by a program you have set up on your computer, such as WordPad or Paint.

You can open and view any shared file from a network computer as long as you have the program that created the file set up on your own computer.

3 Close all open windows.

 TIP If you want to copy a file from another computer onto your computer, use My Computer, Network Neighborhood, or Windows Explorer to click the file, and then on the Edit menu, click Copy. Click folder on your computer's disk drive where you want to copy the file, and then on the Edit menu, click Paste. You can also drag the file to copy it from the other computer to your disk drive.

Disconnect a mapped drive

If you decide you no longer need a network drive, you can disconnect it as easily as you connected it. In this exercise, you'll disconnect a mapped network drive.

1 Open My Computer.

2 Be sure that the toolbar appears on your My Computer window. If the toolbar is not showing, on the View menu, click Toolbar.

Disconnect Net Drive

3 On the toolbar, click the Disconnect Net Drive button.

The Disconnect Network Drive dialog box appears.

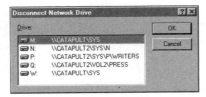

4 From the list of mapped drives, click Drive W, and then click OK.

Be sure to select only the drive you want to disconnect before you click OK. The Drive W icon disappears from the My Computer window.

 TIP In addition to using the toolbar buttons, you can map and disconnect network drives by using the right mouse button to click the Network Neighborhood icon. On the pop-up menu, click Map Network Drive or Disconnect Network Drive.

Making Information Available to Others

You can make information you have on your computer available to others on your network. If your network uses a *server*, you can copy your files to that computer, just like you're copying them to another drive. After you have copied your files to the server, users on your network can view or edit the files.

If your network connects all computers to one another, rather than to a server, you can make information on your computer available to others. When you designate a shared folder on your computer, another user on your network can connect or map to your computer and then view or edit the contents of the shared folder.

You can control which folders are available to other network users. Folders available to other network users are called *public folders*. Folders not available to others are called *private folders*.

You can set access on your folders as *read-only* or *full access*. If your folder is read-only, users on the network will only be able to open and read the files in your shared folder, and they will not be able to change its contents. If your folder has full access, other users will be able to open and read as well as edit its files.

You can add another level of security to your shared files by setting *passwords*. If you want only a few individuals to have full access to a certain folder, you can set a password on that folder. Only those few individuals who know the password will have full access. You can also set a separate password for read-only access. You can establish several combinations of privileges and passwords as you feel is necessary. You can also have no passwords at all.

 NOTE The exercises in this section assume that your network is configured for Share-Level Security, which is the default security setup for Windows 95. For more information about your network's security setup, check with your network administrator.

Copy a file to a server

Let's say you work on a network computer system that uses shared resources, including a server. In this exercise, you'll copy a file to another computer on your network to make it available to other network users.

1 Using either My Computer or Windows Explorer, open the Windows 95 Practice folder.

2 In the Windows 95 Practice folder, click the History file once to select it.

3 On the Edit menu, click Copy.

4 On the taskbar, click My Computer.

5 Open any shared network drive currently connected to your computer.

   If there are no shared network drives mapped to your computer, see the exercise earlier in this lesson entitled "Map to a network drive."

6 On the Edit menu of the shared network drive, click Paste.

   The History file is copied to the network server. Now other users on the network can open the file.

7 Close all open windows.

NOTE Certain networks do not handle long filenames. If you copy a file with a long filename across a network that uses the eight-character filename limit, the long filename will be shortened to eight characters.

Identify a folder as a shared resource

Suppose you want to identify a folder for public use on the network. In this exercise, you'll set a folder as a shared resource for other users on the network to use.

NOTE This exercise works only if your network uses a File and Print Sharing service. To check whether you have this service, use the right mouse button to click the Network Neighborhood icon, and then click Properties. In the Network dialog box, click File And Print Sharing, and then review and select your options.

You can also use the right mouse button to click the folder. Then, from the pop-up menu, click Sharing.

1 Using either My Computer or Windows Explorer, open the hard drive (C:). Click the Windows 95 Practice icon once to select the folder.

2 On the File menu, click Sharing.

3 In the Windows 95 Practice Properties dialog box, click Shared As.

This dialog box might look different, depending on your network properties access and share options.

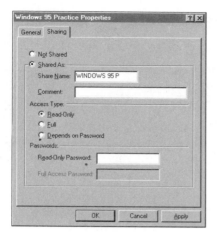

4 In the Comment text box, type **Windows 95 SBS Practice Files**

5 Under Access Type, click Depends On Password.

Under Passwords, both the Read-Only Password and Full Access Password text boxes become available, which you could use if you wanted to use passwords.

6 Under Access Type, click Read-Only, and then leave the Password area blank.

Users will be able to access this folder on your computer without a password, but they will only be able to view the information. They will not have the privilege to change anything.

7 Click OK.

The Windows 95 folder icon changes to indicate that the folder is now a shared resource.

Shared resource

8 Close all open windows.

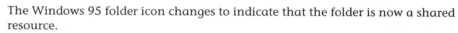

TIP You can also use this procedure to share disk drives. All disk drives and folders are set as private resources until you change them to shared resources.

Sending Messages with Microsoft Exchange

Some features of Microsoft Exchange are only available with additional software.

In Windows 95, Microsoft Exchange replaces Microsoft Mail used with Windows 3.1. However, Microsoft Exchange does much more than handle mail. You can think of Microsoft Exchange as your computer's "post office." Microsoft Exchange manages all of your telecommunication business. It files any incoming messages, whether they are mail messages, fax messages, online service messages, Internet mail, or files. Microsoft Exchange also stores copies of your outgoing messages for your future reference. It alerts you when you have messages that you have not yet read.

You can use Microsoft Exchange to send a mail message to another computer user. In addition, you can send and receive entire files. You can use Microsoft Exchange by double-clicking the Inbox icon on your Desktop.

Send a mail message

In this exercise, you'll send a mail message to yourself using Microsoft Exchange.

 NOTE This exercise works only if you are set up to exchange mail with other users, either on a network or through modem connections. If you are not set up to exchange mail with other users, you can skip to the next exercise.

Inbox (Microsoft Exchange)

If you see the Microsoft Exchange Setup Wizard, it means you still need to specify your communication choices. Follow the Wizard to complete your Microsoft Exchange Profile. For more information, see "Choosing Your Installation Options" in the Appendix.

1 On your Desktop, double-click the Inbox icon to display a special Microsoft Exchange version of Windows Explorer. If your screen does not look similar to the following, be sure that on the View menu, Folders, Toolbar, and Status bar are all checked.

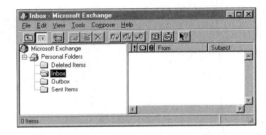

2 On the Compose menu, click New Message to display the New Message window.

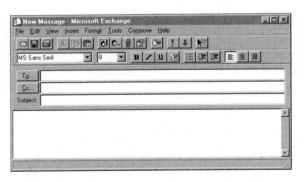

3   In the To box, type your mail user name. If you want, you can type another user name as well.

This will cause your mail message to be sent back to you, just for practice.

4   In the Subject box, type **Testing Microsoft Exchange**

5   In the message area, type the following message:

I am testing Mail and Microsoft Exchange in Windows 95.

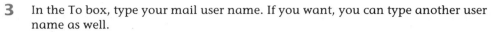

Send

6   On the toolbar, click Send.

Your message is sent to you. It is also sent to any other user you might have specified.

Check for messages

Suppose you want to check and see whether you've received any mail messages or faxes. In this exercise, you'll use Microsoft Exchange to check for incoming messages.

1   With the Microsoft Exchange window still open, double-click the Personal Information Store in the left window.

In the left and right windows, four folders appear. Any folder containing a new, unread message is highlighted. Because you have a mail message waiting for you, your Inbox should be highlighted.

2   In either the left or right window, double-click the Inbox.

The contents of your Inbox appear. Any unread messages are highlighted.

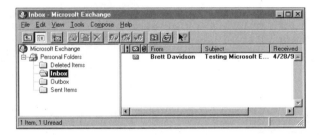

You can also check for messages by clicking Microsoft Exchange on the Programs menu.

3   If you did the mail exercise earlier, you should see a message titled "Testing Microsoft Exchange." Double-click this message.

The message opens in a message window.

4   Close the message window.

The message is no longer highlighted.

5   Close all open windows.

Working with Computers Across Phone Lines

You can use telephone lines to connect to other computers. You might want to connect to a home computer from your work computer. Or, while traveling, you might want to connect to your office computer so that you can access shared files in your company's network. You could also connect to an online service, which is a computer subscription service.

To use telephone lines to connect to other computers, you must have a *modem* as part of your computer hardware. A modem is a device that converts computer information into signals that can be sent across telephone lines. Internal modems are installed inside your computer case, and external modems are separate boxes that connect to your computer by a cable. The computer you're calling must also be connected to a modem so that it can translate the telecommunication signal back into computer information. Any computer with a modem and telecommunication software can send information to other computers and receive information from other computers.

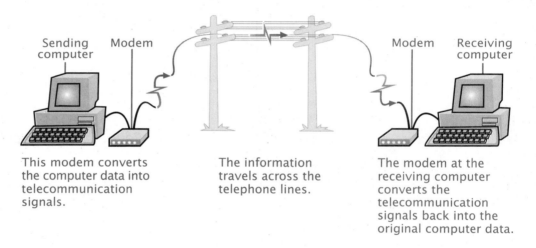

Sending computer   Modem   Modem   Receiving computer

This modem converts the computer data into telecommunication signals.

The information travels across the telephone lines.

The modem at the receiving computer converts the telecommunication signals back into the original computer data.

 NOTE The exercises in this section work only if you have a modem installed as part of your computer hardware. If you do not have a modem, you can skip the following sections and go on to "Finish the lesson."

Calling Another Computer with Dial-Up Networking

You can use Dial-Up Networking to have your computer call another Windows 95 computer. Both systems must have Dial-Up Networking and modems, and the computer you are calling must have the dial-up server software. This is particularly useful if you have a Windows 95 computer with a modem at home as well as at your office. From your home computer, you can use Dial-Up Networking to dial in and connect to your office computer.

This is also useful if there is another Windows 95 computer at your workplace that is storing information you need. If that computer is configured as a dial-up server, you can call that computer and access the information. You might also want to use Dial-Up Networking to print the files in your computer on a printer connected to another Windows 95 computer. This is particularly useful if the printer is not a part of your network.

NOTE If you want to call a computer running a different operating system, for example Windows 3.1 or a computer bulletin board system, use HyperTerminal, as described later in the section "Setting Up a HyperTerminal Connection."

Set up the Dial-Up Networking connection

Suppose you want to set up a Dial-Up Networking connection between your office computer and your home computer. In this exercise, you'll set up the Dial-Up Networking connection so that it's always available for you to use.

1 Open My Computer.

You can also click Dial-Up Networking on the Accessories menu.

2 In the My Computer window, double-click the Dial-Up Networking folder.

The Dial-Up Networking window appears.

3 In the Dial-Up Networking window, double-click Make New Connection.

The Make New Connection window appears.

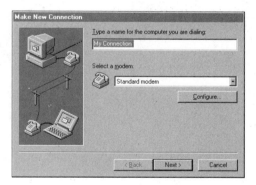

4 Type **My Home Computer** in the Computer Name text box.

This will be the name you'll use every time you make a call with this computer.

5 In the Modem list box, select your modem, and then click Next.

6 In the next window, type your area code in the Area Code box, type **555-1111** in the Telephone Number text box, and then click Next.

This is a "dummy" phone number, for practice only. If you want, you can use an actual modem phone number in this exercise.

7 In the next window, click Finish.

A new icon named "My Home Computer" appears in the Dial-Up Networking window.

 TIP If you need to set up your communication parameters for calling another computer, click Configure next to the Modem list box. In the Modem Properties dialog box, you can set the communication port, speed, data bits, parity, and stop bits so that they match between the two computers. The *communication port* indicates which connector your modem is using. The maximum speed at which your computer can send and receive information is listed in bits-per-second (bps). The rest of these parameters are settings modems use to define how they'll send and receive information. These settings need to match for the two modems to be able to communicate with each other.

Call another computer with Dial-Up Networking

Now that you have set up the connection between your home computer and your office computer, suppose you want to actually dial another computer. In this exercise, you'll call another computer with Dial-Up Networking.

 NOTE For Dial-Up Networking to work successfully, the Dial-Up Networking connection must be set up and active on both computers. To set up your computer as a dial-up server, additional software is required.

1 Be sure that the computer you are calling is turned on. The corresponding connection should be open and ready to receive the call.

If you're using the dummy number (555-1111), you can skip this step for now.

2 With the Dial-Up Networking window still open, double-click the My Home Computer icon to display the Connect To dialog box.

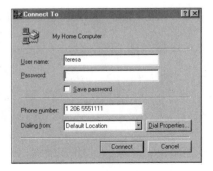

3 Click Connect.

Your computer dials the other computer's phone number. If you're using the dummy number, you'll hear the phone number being dialed, and then you'll hear a recorded message saying that the number is not in service. In this case, click Cancel.

4 Close all open windows.

Setting Up a HyperTerminal Connection

In Windows 3.1, there was a program called Terminal, which you might have used to call other computers. In Windows 95, HyperTerminal is the new version of Terminal. You can use HyperTerminal to connect to computers, particularly computers that are running operating systems other than Windows 95.

You can use HyperTerminal to call and log on to an online service. An *online service* is a subscription computer service you can use to call a computer and access a wide variety of information and talk with thousands of other users. With an online service, you can obtain information on news, sports, weather, the stock market, and more. You can research information on specific topics through hundreds of libraries and databases. You can send mail to other users of the online service. You can chat with other users who are logged on to the service at the same time. You can join topical forums to find information on and discuss issues pertaining to your special interests.

Examples of online services include CompuServe, America Online, and Delphi. In fact, Windows 95 comes with a built-in online service—The Microsoft Network (see "Getting Connected with The Microsoft Network" later in this lesson). Through such an online service, you can access the *Internet*, a collection of computer networks that connects many different online services and computer networks throughout the world.

You can use HyperTerminal to call and log on to a bulletin board service. A *bulletin board service (BBS)* is a computer service that is usually set up for a special interest of some kind. There are many types of bulletin board services set up specifically to provide certain types of technical information, job searches in a particular field, information on a professional organization, and so on. Members who call the bulletin board service can read and send messages, do research on a common database in the bulletin board service, post and read general announcements, and more. A bulletin board service is similar to an online service, but usually has a narrower, more specific scope with a defined membership. Often the service is free. You can connect to the bulletin board service by calling the designated BBS computer.

 NOTE If you want to use files and printers on another computer running Windows 95, use Dial-Up Networking rather than HyperTerminal. See the section earlier in this lesson entitled "Calling Another Computer with Dial-Up Networking."

Connect to another computer with HyperTerminal

Suppose you want to call a computer bulletin board service. In this lesson, you'll set up your modem connections and call the Microsoft Download Service. This free bulletin board service provides application notes, drivers, and other files in support of Microsoft Windows, Word, Excel, Works, BASIC, DOS, and other Microsoft products. The bulletin board also provides new product information and other news items of interest to Microsoft software product users.

Hypertrm

1 Click Start. Point to Programs, point to Accessories, and then click HyperTerminal.

The HyperTerminal window appears.

2 Double-click the Hypertrm icon.

The New Connection - HyperTerminal window appears, and then the Connection Description dialog box appears. Your screen should look similar to the following illustration.

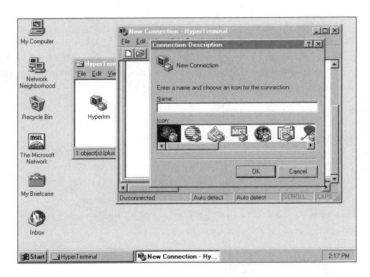

3 In the Name box, type **Microsoft Download Service** (the name for your new modem connection).

4 In the Icon list box, click the first icon.

This icon will represent the Microsoft Download Service in the HyperTerminal window, as will the name you have specified. There are different types of icons available that you can choose to match the type of work you're doing with that computer connection.

5 Click OK.

The Phone Number dialog box appears, as shown in the following illustration.

In this dialog box, you can enter all necessary information regarding the country code, area code, phone number, and your modem communication port.

6   In the Area code text box, type **206**

7   In the Phone Number text box, type **936-6735** and then click OK.

This number is in Washington State, and you will have to pay for this call. If you prefer to use a "dummy" phone number, for practice only, you can type **555-2222** and then click OK.

8   In the Connect dialog box, click Dial.

Through your modem's speaker, you might hear the phone number being dialed, and then the connection will be made to the other computer. In the HyperTerminal window, the message "Welcome to the Microsoft Download Service" appears. If you used the "dummy" phone number, you'll hear a recorded message saying that the number is not in service.

9   Follow the prompts regarding the Microsoft Download Service until the Microsoft Download Service Main Menu appears and then, at the Command prompt, type **E** to exit.

The Microsoft Download Service disconnects.

If you need to enter an access number such as "1" or "9," click Dialing Properties in the Connect dialog box, and fill in the How I Dial From This Location area.

TIP   You can find the names, numbers, and descriptions of other computer bulletin board services in your local computer newspaper or in your favorite computer magazines.

Save the HyperTerminal connection settings

Suppose you expect to dial in to this bulletin board every couple of days, and you want to be able to do this without having to type in the phone number and other communication settings each time. In this exercise, you'll save your connection settings as a file.

1   On the File menu of the Microsoft Download Service-HyperTerminal window, click Save.

The Microsoft Download Service settings are saved as a file.

2   Close the Microsoft Download Service-HyperTerminal window.

The Microsoft Download Service icon appears in the Hypertrm window. Now, anytime you want to make the connection, you can double-click this icon, and then click Dial.

3   Close all open windows.

Getting Connected with The Microsoft Network

The Microsoft Network is an online service with direct access built into Windows 95. You can connect to The Microsoft Network to find the latest news, sports, weather, and financial information. You can exchange messages with other users and obtain answers to technical questions. You can copy, or *download*, software programs from The Microsoft Network computer to your computer and gain easy access to the Internet.

 NOTE   To connect to The Microsoft Network, you must have a modem installed as part of your computer hardware. If you do not have a modem, skip the following sections and go to "Finish the lesson." If you have a modem but do not see the Microsoft Network icon, refer to "Changing Your Setup" in the Appendix.

Obtain introductory information for The Microsoft Network

In this exercise, you'll receive introductory information about The Microsoft Network. This exercise will not cost you anything or obligate you to the online service subscription. You'll just connect briefly to the online service to transfer some information about it to your computer. You can decide later whether you want to join. Only then will you be paying the subscription fee.

The Microsoft
Network

1   Double-click The Microsoft Network icon on your Desktop.

2 Click OK.

A second window appears.

3 Type the requested telephone number information, and then click OK.

The Calling window appears.

4 In the Calling window, click Connect.

Your modem calls and connects to The Microsoft Network. Be patient, The Microsoft Network is downloading introductory information to your computer, and this might take a couple minutes, depending on the speed *(baud rate)* of your modem. The taskbar shows that your modem is working during this time. When all the necessary files have been transferred, a new window appears with three buttons.

Start to sign up for The Microsoft Network

In this exercise, you'll provide certain information required for registering for The Microsoft Network.

1 Click the button next to "Tell Us Your Name And Address."

A personal information form appears, as shown in the following illustration.

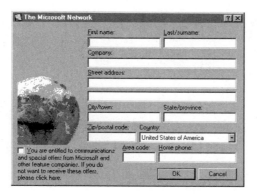

2 Complete the boxes, and then click OK.

3 Click the button next to "Next, Select A Way To Pay."

Another form appears, that lets you choose among three types of credit cards and asks you for the card number and expiration date.

4 Complete the boxes, and then click OK.

You are not obligated until you actually choose to join The Microsoft Network.

5 Click the button next to "Then, Please Read The Rules."

The Microsoft Network Rules window appears.

6 Read the rules, and then click the I Agree button.

Join The Microsoft Network

In this exercise, you'll learn how to join The Microsoft Network.

 IMPORTANT If you do not want to join The Microsoft Network, do not follow these steps. In The Microsoft Network window, click Cancel. You can then skip to "Finish the lesson."

1 If you decide you want to join The Microsoft Network, click Join Now.

If you join, the access phone numbers for your area are displayed in the window.

2 Click OK.

3 In the next window, click Connect.

Once your computer is connected, The Microsoft Network will copy (*upload*) your account information from your computer to the The Microsoft Network computer. You'll now be registered as an official subscriber to The Microsoft Network.

Finish the lesson

In the following steps, you will return your computer to the settings it had when you started this lesson. You will also close any open windows.

1 Using either My Computer or Windows Explorer, open the shared network drive into which you copied the History file. Delete the History file by dragging the file from its network location to Recycle Bin.

 WARNING Be sure to delete only the History file from the network drive. If you have any doubts about the file you should delete, contact your network administrator.

2 Using either My Computer or Windows Explorer, open the hard disk (C:) and click the Windows 95 Practice folder. On the File menu, click Sharing. In the Sharing tab, click Not Shared, and then click OK.

3 In the My Computer window, double-click the Dial-Up Networking folder. Click the My Home Computer icon. On the File menu, click Delete, and then click Yes.

4 On the Start menu, point to Programs, point to Accessories, and then click HyperTerminal. Click the Microsoft Download Service icon. On the File menu, click Delete, and then click Yes.

5 Close all open windows by clicking the Close button in the upper-right corner of each window.

6 If any window is minimized, use the right mouse button to click the window's taskbar button, and then click Close.

You are now ready to start the Review & Practice, or you can work on your own.

7 If you are finished using Windows 95 for now, on the Start menu click Shut Down, and then click Yes.

Lesson Summary

To	Do this	Button
Make a synchronized copy of files and folders with My Briefcase	Drag the file or folder to the My Briefcase icon.	
Copy My Briefcase to a floppy disk	Using My Computer or Windows Explorer, drag the My Briefcase icon to the floppy disk drive icon.	
Use My Briefcase files on another computer	Insert the floppy disk, open the drive, and drag the My Briefcase icon from the floppy disk drive to an empty area on the Desktop.	
Update files between your computer and My Briefcase	Open My Briefcase. On the Briefcase menu, click Update All.	
Set a folder or file on your computer as a shared resource for the network	In My Computer or Windows Explorer, click the folder or file you want to share. On the File menu, click Properties. Click the Sharing tab, and then click Shared As. Set the Access Type. Click OK.	
Map a network drive	On the My Computer toolbar, click the Map Network Drive button. In the Drive box, type the drive letter, and then type or select the path to the computer and folder on the network. Click OK.	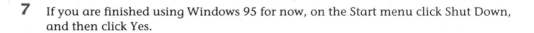
Open and browse through a mapped network drive	In My Computer, double-click the network drive's icon. The shared folders and files on that drive appear.	
Open and browse through Network Neighborhood	Double-click the Network Neighborhood icon. Double-click Entire Network or any computer icons that appear.	
Disconnect a mapped drive	Open My Computer. On the My Computer toolbar, click the Disconnect Net Drive button. Click the name of the network drive you want to disconnect, and then click OK.	

To	Do this	Button
Send a mail message with Microsoft Exchange	Double-click the Inbox icon. On the Compose menu, click New Message. Fill in the message, and then click Send.	
Check Microsoft Exchange for messages	Double-click the Inbox icon. Double-click the items to read them.	
Set up a Dial-Up Networking connection	Double-click My Computer, and then double-click the Dial-Up Networking folder. Double-click Make New Connection. Complete the Dial-Up Networking wizard.	
Call another computer with Dial-Up Networking	Be sure that the computer you are calling is on and the connection is open. In My Computer, double-click Dial-Up Networking. Double-click the icon for the connection, and then click Connect.	
Connect to another computer with HyperTerminal	On the Accessories menu, click HyperTerminal Connections. Double-click HyperTrm. Type a connection name, select an icon, and then click OK. Enter the phone number, click OK, and then click Dial.	
Save the HyperTerminal connection settings	On the File menu of the HyperTerminal window, click Save.	
Dial a saved HyperTerminal connection	In the HyperTerminal window, double-click the connection icon, and then click Dial.	
Sign up for The Microsoft Network	Double-click The Microsoft Network icon, and then click OK. Follow the instructions on the succeeding windows.	

For online information about	From the Help dialog box, click Index and then type
Using My Briefcase	**Briefcase**
Connecting to other computers with HyperTerminal	**HyperTerminal**
Registering for and using The Microsoft Network	**The Microsoft Network**

For online information about	From the Help dialog box, click Index and then type
Sending mail messages with Microsoft Exchange	**mail, exchanging by using Microsoft Exchange**
Setting up and sending faxes with Microsoft Exchange	**fax**
Calling other computers with Dial-Up Networking	**Dial-Up Networking**
Mapping and disconnecting a network drive	**mapping**
Browsing through a network drive	**network**
Sharing drives, folders, or files on the network	**sharing**

For more information on	In *Introducing Microsoft Windows 95*, see
Using Briefcase	Chapter 3, "The Possibilities"
Using the network	Chapter 2, "Beyond the Basics"
Communicating with others	Chapter 3, "The Possibilities"

Review & Practice

In the lessons in Part 3, "Organizing and Communicating Your Work," you learned skills to help you set up and maintain your computer filing system, find files, and work with other computers across telephone lines and networks. If you want to practice these skills and test your understanding, you can work through the Review & Practice section following this lesson.

Review & Practice

Estimated time
25 min.

You will review and practice how to:

■ Organize and manage your files and folders.

■ Synchronize duplicate files with My Briefcase.

■ Find files stored throughout your computer system.

■ Connect to another computer through telephone lines.

■ Send a mail message and check for incoming messages.

■ Map and browse through a network drive.

You can practice the skills you learned in Part 3 by working through the steps in this Review & Practice section. You'll set up and manage a computer filing system, locate files throughout the computer system, and work with other computers across telephone lines or a network.

Scenario

You have been working with your computer for a while and, as a result, you have a number of files associated with different projects. You are now ready to organize and clean up your filing system. In addition, the computers in your company have been set up on a network. Employees in your company now regularly send each other electronic mail and share folders and files. Each computer has also been set up with modem capabilities.

Step 1: *Organize Your Hard Disk*

In this step, you'll create new folders that reflect your file organization scheme, and then move the appropriate files into the folders.

1 In the Windows 95 Practice folder, create the following new folders:

Professional Development

Benefits

2 Move the following files into the indicated folders.

Move this file	To this folder
Brown Bag Presentations	Professional Development
Brown Bag Lunch	Professional Development
Toys Memo	Product Line
Product Table	Product Line
New Employees Report	Benefits
Retirement Planning	Benefits

3 Rename the following files as indicated.

In this folder	Rename this file	To this
Professional Development	Brown Bag Lunch	Brown Bag Graphic
Professional Development	Brown Bag Presentations	Brown Bag Flyer
Benefits	Retirement Planning	Stock Option Plan
Product Line	1996 ProductLine	Childs Play Catalog

4 In the Windows 95 Practice folder, delete the 1990 Employee List.

5 Close all open windows.

Step 2: *Synchronize Files with My Briefcase*

Having reorganized your files on your hard disk, some of them no longer match the corresponding files in My Briefcase. In this step, you'll update the My Briefcase files.

1 Open My Briefcase, and view which files need updating.

2 Update each of the files as required to synchronize the files in My Briefcase with the changes on the corresponding files on your hard disk.

Step 3: *Find Document and Program Files*

You need to work on specific files you know are stored somewhere on your hard disk, but you don't remember their exact names or locations. In this step, you'll use the Find command to find the files indicated in the following steps.

1   You have a graphics file for the brown bag lunch presentations. You have just
    renamed and moved the file, and you're not sure where it is. Find and open the
    graphic. (Hint: Search by name or file type.)

2   You have a letter regarding the conference for customer representatives somewhere
    on your hard disk, but you don't remember its exact name or the folder in which it
    is stored. Find and open the letter. (Hint: Search by the word "conference" or by file
    type.)

3   You know you have the Backup accessory installed on your system, but you don't
    know where it is. Use the Find command to find and start the program.

4   Close all open windows.

Step 4:   *Connect to Another Computer by Phone*

In this step, you'll set up a connection and call another computer to log on to its bulletin
board.

NOTE   This exercise works only if you have a modem as part of your computer hardware. If you do not have a modem, you can skip this exercise.

1   Open the HyperTerminal folder.

2   Create a new connection to the Practice Bulletin Board at phone number 555-3333.
    Assign an icon for the new connection. (Hint: Open Hypertrm.)

3   Dial the new computer connection, and then cancel it.

4   Save the new connection.

5   Close all open windows.

Step 5:   *Send Mail and Check for Messages*

In this step, you'll send a mail message, and then check for incoming mail messages in
Microsoft Exchange.

NOTE   This exercise works only if you are set up to exchange mail with other
users, either on a network or by modem connections. If you are not set up to
exchange mail with other users, you can skip to the next exercise.

1   Use Microsoft Exchange to send the following mail message. Address it to another
    user in your system, if possible, and send yourself a copy as well. (Hint: Use the
    Compose menu.)

    Hi there!
    This is a test for Mail and Microsoft Exchange in Windows 95.
    Thanks for your time!

2 Check for any incoming mail, faxes, or online service messages. (Hint: Use the Personal Folders.)

3 Open and read the mail you sent yourself earlier in Step 1.

4 Close all open windows.

Step 6: *Map to and Open Files on a Network*

In this step, you'll map to another computer drive on your network. You'll also browse through and open shared files available on that computer.

 NOTE This exercise works only if your computer is a part of a network. If your computer is not on a network, you can skip this exercise.

1 Map any available computer and folder on your network to the next available drive on your computer. (Hint: Use the Map Network Drive button on the My Computer toolbar.)

2 Open the mapped network drive and browse through the available folders and files.

3 Find and open a document on the network drive that was created by a program you have installed on your computer, such as a WordPad or a Paint file.

Finish the Review & Practice

In the following steps, you will return your computer to the settings it had when you started this Review & Practice section. You'll also close any open windows.

1 Double-click the My Briefcase icon. If you see the Product Line folder and Product Table file, drag them to the Recycle Bin icon.

The items are deleted from My Briefcase.

2 On the Start menu, point to Programs, point to Accessories, and then click HyperTerminal. Click the Microsoft Download Service icon. On the File menu, click Delete, and then click Yes.

3 Close any documents you opened from the network drive, and then disconnect the mapped network drive.

4 Close all open windows by clicking the Close button in the upper-right corner of each window.

5 If any window is minimized, use the right mouse button to click the window's taskbar button, and then click Close.

You are now ready to work on your own.

6 If you are finished using Windows 95 for now, on the Start menu click Shut Down, and then click Yes.

Appendix

Installing Windows 95

In the Appendix you will learn how to:

- Prepare your system before installing Windows 95.
- Install Windows 95 on a variety of system configurations.
- Change your setup after installing Windows 95.
- Configure your system to match the exercises in this book.

If you have Microsoft Windows 3.1 or Microsoft Windows for Workgroups 3.11 running on your computer, the Appendix will guide you through upgrading to Microsoft Windows 95. If you already have Windows 95 set up on your computer, you might need to set up your printer or additional applications to work with Windows 95. The Appendix will cover several important aspects about setting up Windows 95. In addition, if your screen does not match an illustration as you work through the exercises in this book, the section "Matching the Exercises" provides guidelines to modify your display settings.

 NOTE For specific setup procedures, see *Introducing Windows 95*, which comes with Windows 95.

Preparing Your System for Windows 95

Before you install Windows 95, be sure that your computer system includes at least the minimum system requirements and that you know your hardware components and current settings. If you're upgrading a computer that has work files stored on the hard disk, make backup copies of these files.

Hardware Required

To run Windows 95, your computer system must have the following components:

- A computer based on the Intel 80386DX, 486, or Pentium microprocessor chip.
- 4 MB of memory minimum (8 MB is recommended for good performance).
- A hard disk with at least 40 MB of free storage space.
- One 3.5-inch high-density floppy disk drive or CD-ROM drive.
- A standard VGA (Super VGA recommended) display adapter, along with a compatible monitor.
- A mouse or other compatible pointing device.

While not absolutely required, you will be able to use Windows 95 more effectively if your computer system includes the additional components described as follows:

For more information about Microsoft Exchange, modems or telecommunications software see Lesson 6, "Communicating with Computers."

- If you're planning to use Microsoft Exchange for sending and receiving electronic mail, faxing documents, accessing online services, or other telecommunication capabilities, your computer should have at least 8 MB of memory for good performance and 4 MB of additional hard disk space. You'll also need a modem and possibly a network card.
- Other optional components include a sound card, CD-ROM drive, and multimedia hardware.

Before You Install Windows 95

After you've verified your hardware requirements, the following additional steps are recommended.

- Note your hardware settings if you want to preserve them in Windows 95. To do this, you could print your AUTOEXEC.BAT and CONFIG.SYS files or save them on a floppy disk, note your hardware settings from Windows Setup (in your Main program group), and note your port, printer, and driver settings, also found in the Main program group. For additional information, refer to your Windows 3.1 or your MS-DOS user's guide.
- Back up all of your important data files. You can also back up your program files.

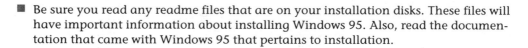

■ Be sure you read any readme files that are on your installation disks. These files will have important information about installing Windows 95. Also, read the documentation that came with Windows 95 that pertains to installation.

Installing Windows 95

Windows 95 is available in the Full Retail product for installing on a blank hard drive or the Upgrade product for installing over a previous version of Windows or other qualifying operating system. You can install Windows 95 using either the installation floppy disks or the installation CD-ROM disc. With either method, you use the Setup program to start the Windows 95 installation process.

If you're installing from floppy disks, the Setup program starts on Disk 1. Note that Windows 95 uses the new *Microsoft Distribution Media Format (DMF)*, which allows more data to be stored on one disk. Because of this format, normal MS-DOS disk commands such as COPY and DISKCOPY will not work on disks numbered 2 and above.

If you're installing from the installation CD-ROM, run the Setup program (Setup.exe) from the Windows 95 installation directory on the CD-ROM.

After you start the installation process, the Setup program will guide you through three distinct phases of installation:

■ Detecting the hardware you have installed on your computer system, and asking you specific configuration questions about your computer system and about how you want Windows 95 to be installed.

■ Decompressing and copying Windows 95 program files from the floppy disks or CD-ROM to your hard disk.

■ Restarting and configuring your Windows 95 system for use.

Installing Windows 95 over Windows 3.1 or Windows for Workgroups 3.11

If you have a previous version of Windows installed on your computer, it is best that you set up Windows 95 from this previous version of Windows using the Upgrade product.

Install Windows 95 over Windows 3.1 or Windows for Workgroups 3.11

1   Insert Disk 1 of your Windows 95 installation floppy disk set into your 3.5-inch high-density floppy disk drive.

Or, if you are using the installation CD-ROM, insert the CD-ROM into your CD-ROM drive.

2   Close any other Windows programs you might have open. Only Program Manager should be running.

3 In Windows 3.1 or Windows for Workgroups 3.11 Program Manager, click the File menu, and then click Run.

The Run dialog box appears.

4 If you are setting up Windows 95 from floppy disks, type the drive designation for your floppy disk drive, type **setup**, and then click OK. For example, if the drive designation for your floppy disk is A:, type **a:\setup** and then click OK to begin the Setup program.

If you are setting up Windows 95 from a CD-ROM disc, type the drive designation for the CD-ROM drive, type **setup**, and then click OK. For example, if the drive designation for your CD-ROM drive is S:, type **s:\setup** and then click OK.

5 Follow the directions throughout the setup process until the installation is complete, following the guidelines in the next section, "Choosing Your Installation Options." As a precaution, select the setup option to back up current Windows files. If you have problems later with Windows 95, you can use the Uninstall feature to return to your original installation.

Choosing Your Installation Options

During the first stage of the installation process, the Setup program will prompt you to choose a Typical, Portable, Compact, or Custom installation. (The lessons in this book assume a Custom installation. See the Custom description that follows.)

The Typical setup installs the standard components of Windows 95, and leaves off options having to do with networks or telecommunication.

The Portable setup installs those components that are useful for laptop, notebook, or other portable computers.

The Compact setup installs only those components that are absolutely essential for Windows 95 to run properly. Use this setup if you have limited disk space.

The Custom setup installs only those components that you specifically select for installation. When you choose a Custom setup, you will see a list of components that you can select or remove from the list of components to be installed on your computer. The lessons in this book assume a Custom installation, with all components installed; therefore, we recommend that you select a Custom setup with all listed components. However, if your computer disk space is limited, you can install only those components required for the lessons you will be working through. The following table lists each lesson in the book and the components required to complete the lesson.

 NOTE You can add or remove components later, after Windows 95 is installed and running, by using the Add/Remove Programs utility in Windows 95 Control Panel. See "Changing Your Setup" later in the Appendix.

For this lesson	You need these components installed
Lesson 1	From the Accessories group: WordPad and Paint.
Lesson 2	From the Accessories group: Charmap, WordPad, Paint, Games, and Wallpaper.
Lesson 3	From the Accessories group: WordPad and Paint.
Lesson 4	From the Accessories group: WordPad, Paint, and Calculator.
Lesson 5	From the Accessories group: WordPad, Paint, and Quick View.
Lesson 6	From the Accessories group: My Briefcase. From the Microsoft Exchange group: Microsoft Mail Services and Microsoft Exchange. From the Communication group: Dial-up Networking and HyperTerminal. From the Microsoft Network group: The Microsoft Network.

During the final stage of the Windows 95 setup process, you will see a series of prompts asking about further setup options, as follows.

- Making a Windows 95 Startup disk. It's a good idea to have a Startup disk handy, in case you ever experience a serious problem with Windows 95 and your system won't start.

- Configuring Microsoft Exchange. If you have telecommunication or mail services installed on your computer, and if you have installed Microsoft Exchange on your computer, you will see the Microsoft Exchange Setup Wizard. Work your way through the Wizard, choosing the information services you'd like to use with Microsoft Exchange, such as Microsoft Mail and Microsoft Fax. Your modem will also be set up in Windows 95 as part of this process.

- Setting up your printer. Although you can set up your printer to work with Windows 95 during this installation process, you can also add or remove printers after Windows 95 is fully installed by using the Printers icon in Control Panel. See the following section, "Changing Your Setup."

Preparing to Use Windows 95

Once Windows 95 is fully installed, configured, and running on your computer system, there are a few more tasks that will make Windows 95 operate according to your expectations.

Registering Your Copy of Windows 95

When you register your copy of Windows 95, you become eligible to receive information and updates regarding Windows 95. Registering also gives you access to Microsoft Product Support Services, which you can call when you have questions about using Windows 95.

There are two ways to register your copy of Windows 95: by completing and mailing the registration postcard that came with Windows 95, or by completing the online registration form and sending it through your modem.

Register Windows 95 online

If your computer system hardware includes a modem, you can register Windows 95 through The Microsoft Network online service.

1　On the Welcome To Windows 95 dialog box, click Online Registration.

　　The Online Registration window appears.

2　Follow the directions in the Online Registration window to register your copy of Windows 95.

Creating the Find Help Database

The first time you use the Find tab in the Help Topics dialog box, you are prompted to create the "lookup list" for the Help files. This list contains every word from your Help files. It's a good idea to create the Find list right after you install Windows 95. This way, when you need to use the Find tab to find a specific Help topic, you won't have to wait for the list to be created.

Load the Find Help database

1　Click Start. On the Start menu, click Help.

　　The Help Topics dialog box appears.

2　Click the Find tab.

　　The Find tab appears, along with a wizard page.

3　Select the best option for your system, and then click Next.

　　The second wizard page appears.

4　Read the wizard page, and then click Finish.

　　Windows 95 creates the search index for your Help files. This process takes a couple of minutes.

For more information on how to use Help, see "Getting Help with Windows 95" in Lesson 1.

5　Click Cancel to close the Help Topics dialog box.

Setting Up Your Windows-Based Programs

If you upgrade your existing Windows 3.1 or Windows for Workgroups 3.11 to Windows 95, you do not need to reinstall your applications. However, if you install Windows 95 to a new directory, so that your previous version of Windows and Windows 95 are installed, then you must reinstall all your Windows-based applications to use them in Windows 95.

When you want to set up a new program for use in Windows 95, you can use one of two methods. With the first method, you use the Run command on the Start menu. You would use the disk drive name that contains the program's setup disk, along with the name of the setup program—for example, Setup or Install.

The Windows 95 Run command is nearly identical to the Windows 3.1 Run command. The program files are decompressed and copied into their own folder on your computer's hard disk. You can find the new folder by browsing Explorer or My Computer, and then you can double-click the main program file to start the program.

The second method to set up a new program is to use Add/Remove Programs in Control Panel. Add/Remove Programs finds the setup program and starts it for you.

 TIP You can add or remove the program startup file to the Start menu, Program menu, or Desktop. Refer to Lesson 2, "Customizing Windows 95" for more information about customizing your menus and creating shortcuts.

Install a Windows-based program

1 Double-click the My Computer icon.

2 In the My Computer window, double-click the Control Panel icon.

3 In the Control Panel window, double-click the Add/Remove Programs icon.

The Add/Remove Programs Properties dialog box appears. Be sure that the Install/Uninstall tab is active, as shown in the following illustration.

Add/Remove Programs

You can also find Control Panel by clicking Start, and then pointing to Settings.

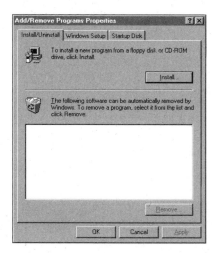

For more information about using Windows-based programs in Windows 95, see Lesson 4, "Working with Your Programs."

4 Click the Install button.

You are prompted to insert the program disk into the disk drive.

5 Find the setup disk (usually Disk 1) of the new application you want to install, and then insert the disk into the appropriate floppy disk drive.

6 Click the Next button.

Add/Remove Programs searches for the installation program on the disk.

7 After it finds the program, click the Finish button.

8 Continue to answer questions about the program setup.

The program is copied to your hard disk. Follow the instructions as directed by the Add/Remove Programs Wizard, until the program is installed on your computer system for Windows 95.

Changing Your Setup

You can make changes to your Windows 95 setup, even after you have finished the Windows 95 installation. You can add and remove Windows 95 program components with Add/Remove Programs. You can add and remove printers with Printers.

Add or remove Windows 95 components

Regardless of which installation option you choose, you can add or remove components later, after Windows 95 is installed and running. You do not have to run the Setup program again. You can add or remove Windows 95 components with Add/Remove Programs in Windows 95 Control Panel. To determine which components are required for each lesson in this book, see "Choosing Your Installation Options" earlier in the Appendix.

1 Double-click the My Computer icon.

You can also find Control Panel by clicking Start, and then pointing to Settings.

2 In the My Computer window, double-click the Control Panel icon.

3 In the Control Panel window, double-click the Add/Remove Programs icon.

The Add/Remove Programs Properties dialog box appears.

4 Click the Windows Setup tab to make it active.

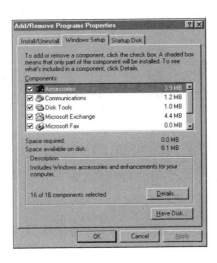

If a component group contains more than one item, you can also click Details and then select the items you want.

5 In the Components list box, double-click a component group, such as Accessories.

The list box displays the detail components in the group. Some groups might only contain one component.

6 Click the check boxes corresponding to the components you want to add or remove. If you are adding a component, you might be prompted to insert one or more of the Windows 95 Setup disks. Follow the directions on your screen to add the component.

A clear check box indicates that the component is not installed or will be removed. A checked box indicates that the component is already installed or it will be added. A grayed box indicates that some, but not all, of the components are installed or will be added.

7 Click OK to return to the Windows Setup tab to select another component group, or click OK to exit Add/Remove Programs.

Install a new printer

You can install a new printer on your computer system to be recognized and used by Windows 95, without running Windows 95 Setup again.

1 Double-click the My Computer icon.

You can also open the Printers window by clicking Start, pointing to Settings, and then clicking Printers.

2 In the My Computer window, double-click the Printers folder.

The Printers window appears. All printers installed with your computer are displayed as named icons.

Printers

3 Double-click the Add Printer icon to display the Add Printer Wizard.

167

4 Read the Add Printer Wizard information, and then click Next.

The second page of the Add Printer Wizard appears.

5 Continue to follow the directions of the Add Printer Wizard to select and add the new printer. You will need to specify the printer model, the port name, and the printer name you want to use. You will also need to insert specified Windows 95 Setup disks to obtain the driver files for your specified printer model.

When you are finished, a new icon appears in the Printers window, indicating your newly installed printer.

6 Close all open windows by clicking the Close button in the upper-right corner of each window.

Matching the Exercises

Windows 95 has many optional settings that can affect either the screen display or the operation of certain functions. Some exercise steps in this book, therefore, might not produce exactly the same result on your screen as is shown in the book. If your screen does not look like an illustration at a certain point in a lesson, a note in the lesson might direct you to the Appendix for guidance. Or, if you do not get the outcome described in the lesson, you can use this Appendix to determine whether the options you have selected are the same as the ones used in this book.

 NOTE Since each computer system is configured with different hardware and software, your screen display of icons, folders, and menu options might not exactly match the illustrations in this book. Such system differences should not interfere with your ability to perform the exercises in the book.

Setting Up Windows 95 Components

The exercises in this book assume a "Custom" setup, with all components installed. If Windows 95 was set up on your computer under a "Typical," "Portable," or "Compact" setup, you might not have all the components necessary to complete the lessons.

If you are missing one or two components, such as an accessory or The Microsoft Network, you can easily add it. For instructions on doing this, see the "Changing Your Setup" section earlier in the Appendix.

If you are missing many components, you might find it easier to re-install Windows 95 under the Custom setup. For instructions on doing this, see the "Installing Windows 95" section earlier in the Appendix. You can run the Windows 95 Setup program from Windows 95.

Using the Default Windows 95 Settings

Windows 95 makes it easy for you to configure your Desktop to suit your working style and preferences. However, the exercises in this book assume that all Windows 95 options are at their default settings. Even when an exercise changes an option setting, the "Finish the Lesson" procedure usually resets the setting to the default.

You can easily change your Windows 95 options to match the illustrations in the exercises.

Show or hide toolbars

You can toggle the toolbar on and off in the My Computer and Windows Explorer windows. The toolbar setting can be different for each window that you open.

1   On the My Computer or Windows Explorer window, click the View menu.

    If the Toolbar command is checked, this indicates that the toolbar is currently showing. If it is not checked, the toolbar is hidden.

2   On the View menu, click Toolbar to show or hide the toolbar.

Change window sizes

If your window sizes appear different from the exercise illustrations, you can change their sizes.

1   Position your mouse pointer on any edge of the window whose size you want to change.

    The mouse pointer changes to a double-headed arrow.

2   Drag the edge of the window in or out to make the window smaller or larger.

Restore windows

If a window is filling the entire screen and you want to see other parts of the Windows 95 Desktop, you can restore the window.

1   Bring the maximized window to the top of your Desktop by clicking its name on the taskbar.

Restore

2   On the maximized window, click the Restore button in the upper-right corner of the window. Be sure that you don't click the Close button to the right of the Restore button.

    The window is restored to its previous, smaller size.

Change views

If you are seeing a different view of files in a My Computer or Windows Explorer window, you can change the view. The views can be different for each My Computer window that you open.

1   In the My Computer or Windows Explorer window for which you want to change the view, click View.

2   On the View menu, click the view you want: Large Icons, Small Icons, List, or Details.

Arrange icons on the Desktop

If your Desktop icons appear jumbled, or in a different order than what you expected to see, you can arrange your icons.

1   Use the right mouse button to click an empty area of the Desktop.
2   On the pop-up menu, point to Arrange Icons, and then click By Name.
    The icons are arranged by name on your Desktop.
3   Use the right mouse button to click an empty area of the Desktop again.
4   On the pop-up menu, point to Arrange Icons, and then click Auto Arrange to arrange your icons.

Arrange icons in My Computer or Windows Explorer

If the icons in a My Computer window or in Windows Explorer appear jumbled, or in a different order than what you expected to see, you can arrange your icons. The icons can have a different arrangement for each window that you open.

1   In the My Computer or Windows Explorer window, click the View menu.
2   On the View menu, point to Arrange Icons, and then click By Name.
    The icons are arranged by name on your Desktop.
3   On the View menu, point to Arrange Icons again, and then click Auto Arrange.

Hide filename extensions in My Computer or Windows Explorer

If the filenames in My Computer or Windows Explorer include three-letter extensions, you can hide the extensions for file types that are registered.

1   In the My Computer or Windows Explorer window, click the View menu.
2   On the View menu, click Options.
3   On the Options dialog box, click the View tab.
4   On the View tab, click Hide MS-DOS Extensions For File Types That Are Registered.
5   Click OK.

Open cascading My Computer windows

If only one My Computer window appears, even as you are opening new folders, you can set your display to open a new window for each new folder.

1   In the My Computer window, click the View menu, and then click Options.
2   In the Options dialog box, be sure that the Folder tab is active.
3   On the Folder tab, click Browse Folders Using A Separate Window For Each Folder.

accessories   Basic programs included with Windows 95 that assist you with your everyday work on the computer, for example, WordPad and Paint. Accessories also include utilities that help you use your computer's telecommunication, fax, and multimedia capabilities more easily. System tools are accessories that help you manage your computer resources. Games are also included as part of your Windows 95 accessories.

application   *See* program.

back up   To create a duplicate copy of files to ensure against loss or damage.

backup disk   A disk that contains information copied from another disk or drive.

baud rate   The speed at which a modem can transmit or receive information. Baud rate can be confused with the more accurate measuring of modem speed in bits-per-second (bps).

bit map   A data structure or method of storing information in memory. Typically, bit map refers to graphic images that are displayed on a computer screen.

bulletin board service (BBS)   A computer service that is usually set up for a specific audience or purpose, such as members of professional organizations or people searching for a job. Members who call the bulletin board service can read and send messages, do research, post and read general announcements, and more.

Calculator   The Windows 95 accessory you can use to perform numeric, scientific, or statistical calculations.

cascading menu   A menu that opens another menu. Cascading menus are indicated by an arrow next to a menu item. By pointing to the item, a new menu opens.

CD-ROM   A compact optical disc, similar in appearance to an audio CD, that can store over 500 MB of read-only information. A CD-ROM drive is needed to read the data on a CD-ROM disc.

Character Map   The Windows 95 accessory that displays available characters in a selected font. It is most often used to insert special symbols into a document that are not easily typed from the keyboard.

Clipboard   The temporary holding place for text or other objects that have been cut or copied in a program.

Clipboard Viewer   The Windows 95 accessory you can use to display the contents of the Clipboard, showing items you have cut or copied while working in programs.

Close button   The button in the upper-right corner of a Windows 95 window that you click to close the window. Closing a program window exits the program.

communication port   Typically, an external connector at the back of a computer system that can be used to connect a modem. *See also* port.

Control Panel   The set of Windows 95 programs you can use to change system, hardware, software, and Windows 95 settings.

Desktop The entire Windows 95 screen that represents your work area in Windows 95. Icons, windows, and the taskbar are displayed on the Windows 95 Desktop. You can customize the Desktop to suit your preferences and working requirements.

destination A document or program into which an object is embedded or linked.

Dial-Up Networking The Windows 95 accessory you use to connect two computers that each have a modem. With Dial-Up Networking, you can share information between the two computers, even if the computers are not on a network.

Documents menu A cascading menu off the Windows 95 Start menu that lists shortcuts to the last 15 document files you opened. When you click a document filename on the Documents menu, the program and the document open.

download To transfer a file from a remote computer to your local computer. This type of transfer can be done with computers on a network or through telecommunication.

electronic mail Notes, messages, and files sent between different computers that use telecommunication or network services. Also referred to as *e-mail*.

embed To insert an object, which is not linked to its originating (or source) document into a destination document. To edit the embedded object, you double-click it to open the source program within the destination document.

Explorer *See* Windows Explorer.

file server *See* server.

folder A container in which document and program files are stored on your disks. Formerly referred to as a *directory*.

format To initialize and prepare a disk for information storage and retrieval. Format also refers to the style of a word processing document.

full access An attribute of a disk volume, folder, or file stored on a shared, network computer that is made available to other users on the network. Full access allows users to make any changes to the volume, folder, or file. *See also* read-only.

graphical user interface A pictorial representation on a computer screen of the files, data, devices, and programs stored on the computer. A user can issue commands to the computer by interacting with the graphic images displayed on the screen.

HyperTerminal The Windows 95 accessory you can use to call another computer, particularly one that runs a different operating system from yours. HyperTerminal is especially useful when you want to log on to an online service or a bulletin board service.

icon A small graphic that represents various Windows 95 elements, including programs, disk drives, and documents. When you double-click an icon, the item the icon represents opens.

Internet   A communication system that connects many different online services and other computer networks throughout the world.

link   To insert information into a destination document that is linked to its source document. When the source document is changed, the linked information is updated.

map   To designate a shared folder or drive on a network computer as a drive available to your computer. When you map a folder or drive, you create a network drive on your computer through which you can use shared resources on the network computer.

Maximize button   The button in the upper-right corner of most windows that enlarges the window to fill the entire screen.

Microsoft Excel   A program you can use to create spreadsheets in which you can store, manipulate, and analyze numerical information.

Microsoft Exchange   The Windows 95 program you can use to send and receive electronic mail, faxes, and files on a network or online service. Microsoft Exchange acts as a central "post office" for all messaging activities.

The Microsoft Network   The built-in online service included with Windows 95. *See also* online service.

Microsoft PowerPoint   A program in which you can combine multiple resources, such as text and graphics, to create attractive, professional slide presentations.

Microsoft Publisher   A desktop publishing program that you can use to design professional quality documents, such as newsletters, brochures, flyers, invitations, and more.

Minimize button   A button in the upper-right corner of most windows. When you click the Minimize button, the window is minimized to its button on the taskbar. The program and document remain open when a window is minimized.

modem   A hardware device that converts digital computer information into audio signals that can be sent through phone lines. These signals are received and converted back to digital signals by the receiving modem.

MS-DOS–based program   A program designed to run under MS-DOS.

My Briefcase   The Windows 95 program you can use to store and synchronize duplicate sets of files and folders between two different computers.

My Computer   The Windows 95 program that you can use to browse through your computer's filing system, and to open drives, folders, and files. You can also use My Computer to manage your files and your filing system, by moving, copying, renaming, and deleting items.

network   A system of multiple computers that uses special networking programs to share files, software, printers, and other resources among the different computers that are connected in the network.

network drive A shared folder or drive on the network that you have mapped to your computer. A network drive is represented by a network drive icon. You can use this icon to open and use the files and folders stored in that drive. *See also* map.

Network Neighborhood The Windows 95 program you can use to explore the network to which your computer is connected.

Notepad A Windows 95 accessory in which you can create short, simple, unformatted documents.

OLE A feature that allows you to import information from a source document into a destination document. The two options for importing are linking and embedding. *See also* link and embed.

online service A subscription computer service that you can use to access information and talk with other users. You can obtain reports on news, sports, weather, the stock market, and more. You can also do research, and send mail to other users of the service.

Paint The Windows 95 accessory that you can use to create, edit, and view computer drawings.

password A unique series of characters that you type to gain entry into a restricted network system, an electronic mail system, or a protected folder or file. Passwords are used to protect the security of the information stored on a computer.

path The location of a file within a computer filing system. The path indicates the disk drive, folder, subfolders, and filename in which the file is stored. If the path indicates a file on another computer on a network, it also includes the computer name.

pel An abbreviation for "pixel."

pixel Short for "picture element." The smallest graphic unit that can be displayed on your screen. All the images displayed on a computer screen are composed of pixels. *See also* bit map.

pop-up menu A menu that lists shortcut commands that directly relate to the action you are performing. Many pop-up menus are accessed by clicking desktop and program elements with the right mouse button.

port A socket or slot that is a connector to your computer system unit into which you can plug the adapter for a hardware device, such as a printer, hard disk, modem, or mouse.

private folder A folder stored on a shared, network computer that has not been designated as available to other users on the network. Only the user who created the folder can open, view, or edit the files in a private folder.

program A detailed set of computer instructions that you can use to perform related tasks, such as composing a letter with a word processing program, calculating a column of figures with a spreadsheet program, or backing up files with a system utility program.

program file A file that stores detailed computer instructions that make a program operational.

public folder A folder stored on a shared, network computer that is made available to other users on the network.

Quick View A resource in Windows 95 that allows you to browse through and view the files on your computer without opening the programs that created each file. Documents can be opened directly from Quick View for editing.

read-only An attribute of a disk volume, folder, or file stored on a shared, network computer that is made available to other users on the network. An item designated as read-only allows users to view files, but not edit the files. *See also* full access.

Recycle Bin The Windows 95 program that holds files, folders, and other items you have deleted. Recycle Bin is represented by an icon on the Desktop. Until Recycle Bin is "emptied," you can recover items you have deleted or placed in Recycle Bin.

Restore button The button in the upper-right corner of a maximized window that restores the window from its maximum size back to its original size.

ScanDisk The Windows 95 accessory that checks a disk or disk drive for faults or errors.

server A central computer on certain types of networks to which all computers on the network are connected, and through which users can obtain shared network resources.

shared resource Hardware, software, or information that users on a network have identified as being available to other users, for example, a public folder, a file server, or a network printer.

shortcut An easily accessible icon that represents and points to a program, folder, or file stored elsewhere on the computer. You can place a shortcut on your Desktop, Start menu, or Programs menu.

shortcut menu *See* pop-up menu.

Start button The command button in the lower-left corner of the Windows 95 Desktop. The Start button serves as the starting point from which all Windows 95 programs, activities, and functions begin.

Start menu The menu that presents commands that are a starting point for all work you do on your computer, such as starting a program, opening a document, finding a file, getting help, and so forth. You open the Start menu by clicking the Start button displayed on the Desktop.

status bar The bar at the bottom of a program window that indicates the program status, for example, the page number, current mode, object size, and so forth. The display of the status bar can often be turned on and off.

synchronize To compare and then update files and folders that are duplicated in My Briefcase and on a computer hard disk. When one of the files in My Briefcase is different from its duplicate stored on the computer hard disk, My Briefcase notifies you and prompts you to update the file, keeping the duplicate files current.

tab dialog box A type of dialog box divided into two or more categories, which can be accessed by clicking the named tabs at the top of the dialog box.

taskbar The rectangular bar usually located across the bottom of the Windows 95 Desktop. The taskbar includes the Start button as well as buttons for any programs and documents that are open. Its location, size, and visibility can be modified to fit your preferences.

toolbox In the Paint accessory, the button box on the left side of the screen that contains tools for adding shapes, text, and other elements to create a drawing.

upload To transfer a file from a user's local computer to a network computer, or to another centrally located computer, perhaps accessed through telecommunication.

Windows-based program A program designed to run on the Windows operating system. *See also* MS-DOS–based program.

Windows Explorer The Windows 95 program you can use to browse through, open, and manage the disk drives, folders, and files on your computer. In a network system, you can also use Windows Explorer to view and open shared folders on other computers on the network. You can use Windows Explorer to manage your files by moving, copying, renaming, and deleting files.

WordPad The Windows 95 accessory you can use to create, edit, format, and view short text documents.

Index

Index

WHO
KNOWS MORE ABOUT
WINDOWS® 95
THAN
MICROSOFT PRESS
?

More Microsoft® Windows® 95

STEP BY STEP

Microsoft Press

ISBN 1-55615-888-2
352 pages
$29.95 ($39.95 Canada)

This is the *Step by Step* guide for you if you have already read MICROSOFT® WINDOWS® 95 STEP BY STEP or UPGRADING TO MICROSOFT WINDOWS 95 STEP BY STEP and would like to learn about the more advanced features of Windows 95. This proven self-paced training package teaches readers to use the new telecommunication, system management, multimedia, and Plug and Play features of Windows 95, plus other new enhancements.

Geared to time-conscious individuals, *Step by Step* books offer excellent self-paced instruction, with timesaving practice files included on disk, follow-along lessons, and practice exercises. They are ideal training tools for business, classroom, and home use.

Microsoft®Press

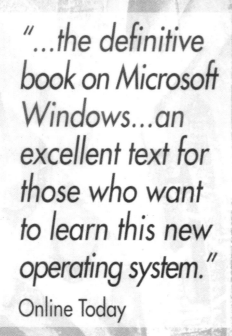

IMPORTANT — READ CAREFULLY BEFORE OPENING SOFTWARE PACKET(S).
By opening the sealed packet(s) containing the software, you indicate your acceptance
of the following Microsoft License Agreement.

Microsoft License Agreement

MICROSOFT LICENSE AGREEMENT
(Single User Products)

This is a legal agreement between you (either an individual or an entity) and Microsoft Corporation. By opening the sealed software packet(s) you are agreeing to be bound by the terms of this agreement. If you do not agree to the terms of this agreement, promptly return the book, including the unopened software packet(s), to the place you obtained it for a full refund.

MICROSOFT SOFTWARE LICENSE

1. GRANT OF LICENSE. Microsoft grants to you the right to use one copy of the Microsoft software program included with this book (the "SOFTWARE") on a single terminal connected to a single computer. The SOFTWARE is in "use" on a computer when it is loaded into temporary memory (i.e., RAM) or installed into permanent memory (e.g., hard disk, CD-ROM, or other storage device) of that computer. You may not network the SOFTWARE or otherwise use it on more than one computer or computer terminal at the same time.

2. COPYRIGHT. The SOFTWARE is owned by Microsoft or its suppliers and is protected by United States copyright laws and international treaty provisions. Therefore, you must treat the SOFTWARE like any other copyrighted material (e.g., a book or musical recording) except that you may either (a) make one copy of the SOFTWARE solely for backup or archival purposes, or (b) transfer the SOFTWARE to a single hard disk provided you keep the original solely for backup or archival purposes. You may not copy the written materials accompanying the SOFTWARE.

3. OTHER RESTRICTIONS. You may not rent or lease the SOFTWARE, but you may transfer the SOFTWARE and accompanying written materials on a permanent basis provided you retain no copies and the recipient agrees to the terms of this Agreement. You may not reverse engineer, decompile, or disassemble the SOFTWARE. If the SOFTWARE is an update or has been updated, any transfer must include the most recent update and all prior versions.

4. DUAL MEDIA SOFTWARE. If the SOFTWARE package contains both 3.5" and 5.25" disks, then you may use only the disks appropriate for your single-user computer. You may not use the other disks on another computer or loan, rent, lease, or transfer them to another user except as part of the permanent transfer (as provided above) of all SOFTWARE and written materials.

5. LANGUAGE SOFTWARE. If the SOFTWARE is a Microsoft language product, then you have a royalty-free right to reproduce and distribute executable files created using the SOFTWARE. If the language product is a Basic or COBOL product, then Microsoft grants you a royalty-free right to reproduce and distribute the run-time modules of the SOFTWARE provided that you: (a) distribute the run-time modules only in conjunction with and as a part of your software product; (b) do not use Microsoft's name, logo, or trademarks to market your software product; (c) include a valid copyright notice on your software product; and (d) agree to indemnify, hold harmless, and defend Microsoft and its suppliers from and against any claims or lawsuits, including attorneys' fees, that arise or result from the use or distribution of your software product. The "run-time modules" are those files in the SOFTWARE that are identified in the accompanying written materials as required during execution of your software program. The run-time modules are limited to run-time files, install files, and ISAM and REBUILD files. If required in the SOFTWARE documentation, you agree to display the designated patent notices on the packaging and in the README file of your software product.

LIMITED WARRANTY

LIMITED WARRANTY. Microsoft warrants that (a) the SOFTWARE will perform substantially in accordance with the accompanying written materials for a period of ninety (90) days from the date of receipt, and (b) any hardware accompanying the SOFTWARE will be free from defects in materials and workmanship under normal use and service for a period of one (1) year from the date of receipt. Any implied warranties on the SOFTWARE and hardware are limited to ninety (90) days and one (1) year, respectively. Some states/countries do not allow limitations on duration of an implied warranty, so the above limitation may not apply to you.

CUSTOMER REMEDIES. Microsoft's and its suppliers' entire liability and your exclusive remedy shall be, at Microsoft's option, either (a) return of the price paid, or (b) repair or replacement of the SOFTWARE or hardware that does not meet Microsoft's Limited Warranty and which is returned to Microsoft with a copy of your receipt. This Limited Warranty is void if failure of the SOFTWARE or hardware has resulted from accident, abuse, or misapplication. Any replacement SOFTWARE or hardware will be warranted for the remainder of the original warranty period or thirty (30) days, whichever is longer. Outside the United States, these remedies are not available without proof of purchase from an authorized non-U.S. source.

NO OTHER WARRANTIES. Microsoft and its suppliers disclaim all other warranties, either express or implied, including, but not limited to implied warranties of merchantability and fitness for a particular purpose, with regard to the SOFTWARE, the accompanying written materials, and any accompanying hardware. This limited warranty gives you specific legal rights. You may have others which vary from state/country to state/country.

NO LIABILITY FOR CONSEQUENTIAL DAMAGES. In no event shall Microsoft or its suppliers be liable for any damages whatsoever (including without limitation, damages for loss of business profits, business interruption, loss of business information, or any other pecuniary loss) arising out of the use of or inability to use this Microsoft product, even if Microsoft has been advised of the possibility of such damages. Because some states/countries do not allow the exclusion or limitation of liability for consequential or incidental damages, the above limitation may not apply to you.

U.S. GOVERNMENT RESTRICTED RIGHTS

The SOFTWARE and documentation are provided with RESTRICTED RIGHTS. Use, duplication, or disclosure by the Government is subject to restrictions as set forth in subparagraph (c)(1)(ii) of The Rights in Technical Data and Computer Software clause at DFARS 252.227-7013 or subparagraphs (c)(1) and (2) of the Commercial Computer Software — Restricted Rights 48 CFR 52.227-19, as applicable. Manufacturer is Microsoft Corporation, One Microsoft Way, Redmond, WA 98052-6399.

This Agreement is governed by the laws of the State of Washington.

Should you have any questions concerning this Agreement, or if you desire to contact Microsoft for any reason, please write: Microsoft Sales and Service, One Microsoft Way, Redmond, WA 98052-6399.

CORPORATE ORDERS

If you're placing a large-volume corporate order for additional copies of this *Step by Step* title, or for any other Microsoft Press book, you may be eligible for our corporate discount.

Call **1-800-888-3303, ext. 62669,** for details.

097-000-681

The
Step by Step
Practice Files Disk

The enclosed 3.5-inch disk contains timesaving, ready-to-use practice files that complement the lessons in this book. To use the practice files, you'll need the Windows 95 operating system.

Each *Step by Step* lesson uses practice files from the disk. Before you begin the *Step by Step* lessons, read the "Getting Ready" section of the book for easy instructions telling how to install the files on your computer's hard disk. As you work through each lesson, be sure to follow the instructions for renaming the practice files so that you can go through a lesson more than once if you need to.

Please take a few moments to read the License Agreement on the previous page before using the enclosed disk.